SCHOOLING
PROBLEMS
SOLVED WITH NLP

SCHOOLING PROBLEMS SOLVED WITH NLP

WENDY JAGO

Featuring CHARLES DE KUNFFY

J. A. ALLEN · LONDON

© Wendy Jago 2001
First published in Great Britain 2001

ISBN 0 85131.786.3

J. A. Allen
Clerkenwell House
Clerkenwell Green
London EC1R 0HT

J. A. Allen is an imprint of Robert Hale Ltd

British Library Cataloguing in Publication Data
A catalogue record for this book is available from the British Library

Photographs on pages 128 (upper), 169, by Sheila Ball, pages 159, 166, by
Kimberley Battleday, pages 61, 73, 119, 128 (lower), 130, 131, 145, 148, 149,
190, 191, 210, 213, 215, 217, 219, by Mick Green. Photograph of Charles de
Kunffy on page 197 reproduced by permission of Horse and Rider.
All other photographs by Charlotte, Leo and Wendy Jago.

Edited by Martin Diggle
Designed by Paul Saunders
Illustrated by Gisela Holstein

Colour separation by Tenon & Polert Colour Scanning Ltd.
Printed in Hong Kong by Dah Hua International Printing Press Co. Ltd.

In loving memory of two generous spirits

Fleetwater Vice Versa – Hawkeye

and

Edna Long, my mother, who first asked
me if I would like to learn to ride

Contents

Acknowledgements

My special thanks are due to Charles de Kunffy and Ian McDermott, the sources of my inspiration; to my teachers Kimberley Battleday and Debby Lush, for helping me transform my riding and take it in the right direction; to the Teachers of Tomorrow Trust, which does so much to promote classical training and was where I first encountered de Kunffy and Kottas; to Karen Broxton and Nikki Green, who have made working together such a delight; to Mick Green, who framed many of the photographs so appropriately; to my publisher, Caroline Burt, who believed in the project and nurtured it at every stage; to my editor, Martin Diggle, who sympathetically oversaw the dotting of the 'i's and the crossing of the 't's; to my designer, Paul Saunders, who has given life and shape to this book; to Leo and Charlotte, as always; and of course to Tristan, Hawkeye, Lolly, Vals and Voyager, without whom…

I would like to thank the following publishers for permission to use material quoted in the text:

Half-Halt Press, for quotations from Charles de Kunffy's *The Ethics and Passions of Dressage*.

Harper Collins, for quotations from Joseph O'Connor and Ian McDermott's *Principles of NLP* and *The Art of Systems Thinking*.

Howell Book House, for quotations from Charles de Kunffy's *Training Strategies for Dressage Riders*.

Metamorphous Press, for the quotation from Moshe Feldenkrais' *The Master Moves*.

Penguin Books, for the quotation from Charles Handy's *Understanding Organisations*.

Real People Press, for the quotations from Leslie Cameron Bandler, David Gordon and Michael Lebeau's *Know How*.

Science and Behavior Books, for the quotation from the quotation from Genie Laborde's *Influencing with Integrity*.

Foreword

Dr Wendy Jago's book, *Schooling Problems Solved with NLP*, is fascinating reading because of its concentration on the complex communications between humans and horses. Beautifully written and easy to comprehend, it makes a profound subject eminently accessible and fabulously utilitarian. Full of examples that all riders at any level of sophistication will recognize, the book also provides abundant and succinctly spelled-out suggestions for problem solving.

For a man singled out for extraordinary praise in the text to call this work excellent in accomplishing what it sets out to do, seems immodest. However, my satisfaction with this extraordinarily interesting book is not animated by immodesty. I would hope that my introduction will be understood as impartial praise. My praise is offered not out of self-interest but because it is earned by Dr Jago.

Schooling Problems Solved with NLP elucidates the premise that the art of riding is based on two living creatures communicating successfully. The success of that communication is proportionate to the rider's level of human insight achieved through love for the horse. It is anchored in the understanding of another living entity through empathy and respect.

Wendy Jago emphasizes the principle that riders must bring to their art talent, well-developed skills and the refinements of their mind. When riding, people display their emotions and they can refine them by acquiring or enhancing their virtues through communicating with horses.

Not only is *Schooling Problems Solved with NLP* a thought-provoking book, but it is also a pleasure to read because it is so well organized. I think this work is indispensable to all teachers of horsemanship. Inasmuch as all riders, by necessity, are their own primary instructors, this emotionally satisfying book will be a most important asset to their learning.

Wendy Jago successfully integrates the complex ideology that is central to my understanding of what an equestrian ought to be: a well-developed evolutionary product of an educated mind, an elevated spirit and a superbly skilled athletic body.

Riding can only be as good as the thinking and emotional context from which it is derived. The physical act of riding is a consequence of thinking and feelings communicated successfully. Wendy Jago's book is explicit in helping to make that goal possible.

CHARLES DE KUNFFY, Pacifica, CA., April 2000

Introduction

We should ride for the joy of the process of harmonious
communication between horse and rider.
CHARLES DE KUNFFY *The Ethics and Passions of Dressage*

The rider's state of mind, emotions and character are all more
important to horsemanship than are specific skills.
CHARLES DE KUNFFY *The Ethics and Passions of Dressage*

Another book about horse-riding? A promise of yet another way to solve riding problems? So what's new… and what is NLP?

Riding depends on communication: my horse and my muscles both have to understand what I want. As we all know, wanting is not always the same as achieving!

This book sets out to show for the first time how the best current understanding of how our minds work and what makes for good communication can be applied to riding, to help committed everyday riders and their horses. That's you and me. The idea for the book came because when I was training to become an NLP Master Practitioner I found that I kept using my new NLP skills to sort out the problems my horse and I were having – and that NLP kept on helping. And the more enthusiastic I became and the more I could point to the differences NLP had made, the more horsy people I knew became interested. And so I started helping them with the problems they had with their horses…

NLP was first developed in the 1970s as a description of how really outstanding communication works: a description at a real nuts-and-bolts level. It grew from this to become the nearest thing we have to a user's manual for human beings: it's practical, factual and user-friendly. It makes sense because it's based on observation and on asking people how they actually do things, not on theories, 'oughts', 'musts' or 'shoulds'. And 'do' means not only how they behave on the outside but how they think or feel on the inside – and also how the two interact.

NLP has a great deal to offer riders on a number of fronts:

1. **When we watch someone really excellent in their field we often ask: *'How do they do that?'*** NLP helps us to ask the kind of questions which give us the exact information we need to answer that question. In riding, this covers a number of areas:
   - body positioning and use;
   - strategies for training and influencing the horse;
   - and, less obvious but very important indeed, what is going on in the mind of the person whose skill we are trying to learn. Not just what they are thinking, but also *how*. Not just how in large-scale terms (e.g. being positive or goal-orientated) but how in small-scale (picturing or feeling, talking to themselves, remembering past successes or imagining future ones). NLP calls this process of gathering information **modelling**.

2. **It helps us understand how our own individual ways of thinking and feeling actually work, and how this can help and hinder us in our riding (and in other things we do).** Stuck patterns, 'can't dos', old fearfulnesses which get in the way can all at last be understood – and changed. NLP helps us discover that failure and underachievement have *structure* – they're not random or accidental, but patterns that get constructed, used and often repeated. Likewise success and confidence. Once we understand the structure we know what needs to be done – or changed.

3. **Once we know the changes we want, NLP offers us effective tools with which to make them.** Outstanding people in many walks of life and many fields of endeavour unknowingly use identical strategies to get what they want. Effectiveness isn't a mystery any more, thanks to the people who developed NLP by being curious in a really detailed way. NLP is based on observation and the identification of common patterns. These patterns are all around us. Often we call them 'instinctive' or 'natural'; but that doesn't mean that they are mysterious or belong only to the people to whom skills and success 'come naturally'. As you read this book you will find some key NLP tools explained, together with suggestions for how they can be used to help your riding.

4. NLP gives us a lot of information about how people make sense of their experience. Things don't just 'happen' to us: events do, but what counts is what we make of them. The everyday phrase I just used – *make sense of* – shows how it is actually common knowledge that we personally transform the events of our lives and make meaning from them. We tell ourselves stories; show ourselves videos in the privacy of our own heads; talk to ourselves and hear others in an internal 'cast of thousands'; we 'feel for' others and are 'weighed down by' things. It's busy in there. NLP helps us understand how we actually do this – and shows us how to work out a lot about how others do it too. Understanding our own personal style in this way means that we can use our strengths more, and know where to work on the things we find difficult.

5. It also helps us understand what our own behaviour may look like from another point of view, teaching us to imagine ourselves into someone else's shoes. This can help us understand how our horses may be experiencing us and our training, and how we can make our relationships with them more harmonious and more effective.

So NLP offers riders a great deal.

NLP stands for **Neuro-Linguistic Programming**: the way people make sense of their experience and the ways this 'sense' is held in the 'languages' of the mind and body. Programming reminds us of computers, which – though far less complex and far less flexible – are the nearest analogy we have to the wonderful workings of the brain. Human beings are creatures of patterns: we notice them in the world around us; we look for them in our experience; we turn them into our own habits of thought and action; we rely on them to help understand the past and predict the future; they are the basis of education and training – of humans and of animals.

We can't function without our programming; but it can also get in the way. Old learning can be the root of limitations and fears. It can prevent us from doing the things we would like to do, both physically and mentally. As a rider, I look enviously at my husband and daughter, both of whom were trained classically from the very beginning: when I began dressage I had to unlearn years of riding-school riding, of legs for start and reins for stop, and years of fearfulness about the possibility of being run away with or falling off.

The first rides I had when I was ten, at a riding school in North London, had a set pattern: hack from the stables through suburban streets to Hampstead Heath, then round a sandy track where we could canter. Like riding school horses everywhere, ours knew where they walked and trotted on the road – and where they started and finished their bursts of canter on the track. Rider instructions were not needed! It was only many years later when I was using NLP to overcome my fear about cantering my young horse that I realised where the fear started. I had learnt from those riding school days not that cantering was dangerous, but that it was *out of my control.* Even at a later riding school I went to on the edge of London, cantering on a local farm still happened at set places and times in the ride, which reinforced my earlier experiences. Though as an adult I 'knew' intellectually that I now had the skill to control my horse's canter with my seat rather than by pulling on the reins, that knowledge didn't help the fear whenever I thought about cantering. And the fear in turn affected the way my body behaved when about to canter. I tipped forward and stiffened, making my fear come true through the change of position and the increase in anxiety. Telling myself I needn't, or ought not to, fear cantering had no effect: I just felt stupid and inadequate (over fifty and frightened of cantering?). But once I knew how my fear had started, and how it was being reawakened each and every time I cantered, I could find the NLP skill that would change things. And the change was immediate – and lasting. Different chapters in the book will explore the influence of the past and the mind-body connection and some useful NLP strategies, including the one that worked for me.

This book is called *Schooling Problems Solved with NLP* because most of us really want to get away from the tensions, anxieties and frustrations we feel when things go wrong and we seem stuck. But because NLP is about pattern-structures, it also helps us discover the structure of *what does work* for us, so we know how to do it again, or do more of it. Like using a good recipe, NLP is a way of knowing how we can reliably get the results we want again and again.

Because it is concerned with the structure of thought and behaviour, NLP offers us ways of understanding what is, and of changing it if we want to. The choice is up to us. NLP is a great tool-kit in many fields: personal insight and development, management, education, training and coaching. It's particularly helpful for activities which involve both mind and body, such as riding and other sports, because it's based on the understanding that mind and body are not separate, but a set of interlocking systems. We can approach riding problems through increased body-awareness and exercises: NLP can help us change well-ingrained physical habits, as many examples in this book show. It can also help us greatly with the difficulties which arise from our attitudes, beliefs, feelings, or past learning. And because it is also about the processes of communication and

Fear affected my body… Wendy with Tristan.

understanding between individuals, it can really help with the problems we have in getting on with – or getting through to – our horses.

As I have explained, NLP teaches us to ask questions about detail. And when we get the detail, it helps us sort out exactly which details are the really crucial ones – what it calls '*the difference that makes a difference*'. When something is a problem for us, we tend to assume that changing it will be hard or will take a long time. If we can find the right detail, the right place to make a change, it can actually be easy and very quick, as you will see from some of the rider examples in this book. That, also, is one of the great strengths of NLP – and it has two bases: first, the brain is incredibly fast; and, second, once we change any part of a pattern (especially if it's a key part) the pattern as a whole will be different. It's rather like those kaleidoscopes full of little bits of coloured glass or plastic. Even the tiniest shake makes an entirely new pattern, though the pieces are the same. But whereas you can't put new pieces into a kaleidoscope, you can put new information into the brain, so we can change old patterns not just by rearranging the pieces, but also by introducing new ones.

NLP is not a set of theories: it is a set of descriptions, so it works, and it tells us what works – and what doesn't. But while it can help us understand how we can bring about our successes and our failures, how we can move on (or make sure that we stay stuck!), it does not make judgements, any more than a do-it-yourself manual does. It tells us about actions and consequences, but it doesn't praise or blame. And this in itself is very helpful, since most of us find it only too easy to blame ourselves when things go wrong.

In fact, NLP goes even further: it tells us that 'failure' is actually information – if we learn to look at it that way. It can give us valuable feedback on the effects of what we did or thought, so that we can do something different next time. So instead of just feeling bad about it when something doesn't work, we can begin to think about how that happened, and what would happen if we altered something – and which would be the best something to alter. Using **failure as feedback** is one of the great transforming ideas of NLP, as some of the examples in the book illustrate.

Another really useful theme of NLP is that the meaning of anything we try to communicate to someone else (human and horse) is not what we intend but *what they think we meant*. Meaning is in the mind of the receiver, not the sender. Again, it is non-judgemental, so it is pointless to get angry about the fact that 'he didn't understand'. If my horse gets a different message from the one I intended, it doesn't make me a bad rider or him a disobedient horse. He certainly understood something; if it wasn't what we wanted, then let's look at what he did seem to understand, work out how he got there, and try another way of putting our original message across so that he does get it next time. Neither of us is to blame. We don't need to waste time and energy being disappointed or angry.

I was judging at an unaffiliated horse trials, and after the dressage was over I went to watch the cross-country and showjumping phases. One horse refused three times at a fence. Although he was clearly going to dig his heels in at the first attempt, at the second and third tries the rider approached the fence in exactly the same way. Because it was a friendly show, the organiser gave her the chance of jumping another fence on the way out, hoping presumably to give her and her horse a successful experience to finish on. Again she hurtled up to the fence with a long run-up; again the horse refused; then the rider whipped him, and hit him again after she left the arena. What was the horse making of these experiences? What was he learning?

Let's take another example. Some years ago, a middle-aged schoolmaster came to live at our yard. We didn't know his history, but when someone went to put his bridle on he seemed terrified, backing away, threatening to rear, trembling and snorting. It took half an hour – and what worked in the end was holding the bridle open just below his nose. Then he opened his mouth willingly and put it onto the bit, and allowed the headpiece to be slipped gently over his ears. We never discovered what he remembered, or feared, but everyone found they could bridle him – provided they did it his way.

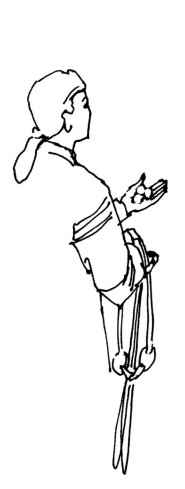

When someone went to put his bridle on, he seemed terrified.

The horse in the first example 'told' the rider he was not willing/ready/happy to take that fence. Something would have to change in order for him to be willing to do so. If the rider had been able to pay attention to his response as information, rather than judging it as 'naughty', 'lazy', 'disobedient' (or whatever negative came into her mind) she might have been able to change her strategy, and perhaps influence him to change his response. More of the same from her, however, just got more of the same from him. There is an NLP saying which exactly describes this: *If you always do what you've always done, you'll always get what you've always got.* The trainer at the yard, on the other hand, attended to the horse's response, and refrained from thinking 'Horses ought to be willing to have a bridle put on', or 'He's difficult in the stable: I'll have to show him who's boss'. She respected the signs of genuine fear the horse was showing, and tried a number of different approaches until she found the one he was able to accept.

We could write these examples out as a kind of dialogue (for that is what they really are).

RIDER: Jump this fence

HORSE: Not on your nelly

RIDER: Go on, jump it

HORSE: No way

RIDER: I TOLD YOU, JUMP IT!

HORSE: nothing doing, mate.

RIDER: Let's put your bridle on

HORSE: I'm frightened

RIDER: I wonder what's frightening you. Would it be better if we did it this way?

HORSE: Not really

RIDER: What about this way?

HORSE: That's no better

RIDER: Look, let me just show it to you

HORSE: If you do it like that I can put it on myself. Thanks.

In this book, I make a number of assumptions about rider-horse interaction which are based on NLP. NLP uses the word **Presupposition** to describe these kind of beliefs which guide our attitudes and behaviour. Presuppositions filter our understanding of what happens so they frequently help to bring about what we are expecting or believing. We can write out what happens like this:

Belief ▶ behaviour in line with belief ▶ response ▶ interpretation of response in line with belief

…which frequently feeds back and reinforces the belief. For example, the presupposition 'horses are naturally lazy':

Horses are naturally lazy
- ▶ my horse is naturally lazy
- ▶ my aiding becomes stronger
- ▶ my horse becomes indifferent or 'dead to the aids'
- ▶ my horse does indeed appear lazy
- ▶ my belief is confirmed.

On the other hand, another rider might have a very different presupposition, 'horses are sensitive but need to have their attention engaged'. This sequence might then go:

Horses are sensitive but need to have their attention engagaed
- ▶ rider's aids are light but she immediately corrects lapses of attention
- ▶ horse learns to respond quickly to light aids
- ▶ rider's belief is confirmed.

Given that presupposing is a natural human activity, it follows that some kinds of presuppositions are more useful and get us further than others. At the end of this chapter is a list of some presuppositions widely held in NLP which I think can be very helpful to us as riders.

Here are the horse-related presuppositions on which I have based this book.

Presuppositions about the horse

1. The horse knows how to be a horse. He knows how to do everything a horse needs to do effectively in terms of his physiology, his survival and his comfort – in the wild. He does not know how to carry a rider with least damage to his muscles, joint and spirit or how to take care of himself in captivity.

2. Through experience, the horse has learnt things about people, his environment and what he is expected to do. He has learnt that behaviour has consequences. He responds to events and his surroundings according to his learning and his individual nature.

3. Comfort, reward, company and stimulus are important to him. He tries to avoid things he expects to be hard or painful.

4. He learns indiscriminately from everything that happens to him or around him.

Presuppositions about the rider

1. Everything we do around our horses communicates something to them.

2. When we ride, everything we do says something to our horse.

3. The response we get tells us the message the horse received.

4. What we allow our horse to do, we allow him to learn: therefore we are in fact unintentionally teaching it to him.

5. What we repeat, we reinforce.

6. If we believe something, that is what our behaviour leads us to get.

7. As riders, we are what we think, feel and believe.

NLP has made a huge difference to me as a rider, and to the other riders I have helped using its tools. I hope that you too will find it helps you in very practical ways in your riding – and in other areas. At the end of the book there are suggestions for other books you might read if you want to know more about NLP as such. This book is about NLP in action in the stableyard, the school and in competition, and it is divided into five sections.

Section One, The Basic Skills for Problem-solving with NLP, introduces and explores how it can help us make our thinking and our actions more effective.

Section Two, Solving Problems in Rider-Horse Communication, looks at common problems that crop up in the relationships between riders and their horses, and how NLP can be used to help.

Section Three, Problems of Muscle and Message, looks at NLP and the physical difficulties we may encounter in riding: first, what to do when we know what we should be doing but cannot do it, and second, the ways our bodies unintentionally give our feelings away, especially when we are under pressure, as in competition.

Section Four, Getting it All Together, looks at ways forward: those two key questions of how we build self-confidence and achieve what we want in our riding.

In all of these sections you'll find horsy examples to illustrate and clarify the points made, and practical exercises and suggestions for applying NLP to your own riding problems and needs.

Finally, **Section Five, NLP at Work,** gives some fuller examples of NLP in action. First, a portrait of Charles de Kunffy, one of the great rider/trainer/writers of our time, showing how NLP helps us understand exactly how he does what he does so effectively. And, second, some short accounts of how NLP helped real, everyday riders to sort out problems they had in their riding.

If you read the book in this order, you will learn some of the major NLP ideas and tools. It is, above all, a practical tool-kit. Like all tools, NLP ones have their own names, and I have given them in bold type when first explaining them. After the initial explanation of what the tool is and how it can be used, it is just referred to by its name when it crops up again.

Above all, my belief in writing this book is that NLP offers all of us as riders many ways to improve our daily communication with our horses, so that we can both enjoy our meetings with freedom, clarity and satisfaction. For this reason, this is a book for everyone who cares about riding, whatever their discipline or the level of their work. The book is about the interaction between horse and rider – the 'conversation' or the 'dance'. It's about a process which happens every time we are together. For example, if you want to achieve more fluent lateral work, these tools will help you do it – but they will do it as a result of something more profound: an improvement in the mutual understanding between you and your horse. Charles de Kunffy has said that while a horse can be a horse without a rider, a rider cannot be a rider without a horse, neither can a horse achieve the most that he is capable of as an athlete without a rider to shape his energies and his form. NLP shows us some important, and exciting, ways to do this. It makes available to all of us, if we pay attention, what the greatest riders have known and done instinctively, what the masters have taught and written: it shows us the HOW.

Some NLP presuppositions which can help us as riders

- People respond to their map of reality, not to reality itself. NLP is the art of changing these maps, not reality.

- Every behaviour has a positive intention and is useful in some context.

- There is no failure, only feedback. Every experience can be utilised.

- Behaviour is the highest quality information.

- Mind and body are one integrated system.

- Programmes are formed from experience, can be triggered automatically, and can be changed.

- Anything can be accomplished by anyone: if one person can do something, it is possible to model it and teach it to others. However, you may need to break the task down into small enough chunks.

- Modelling leads to excellence.

- You cannot not communicate. You are always communicating in all three major representational systems – visual, auditory and kinesthetic (physical experience).

- Communication is both verbal and non-verbal, both conscious and unconscious.

- The meaning of the communication is the response it elicits.

- There is no resistance – only inflexible communicators. Resistance is a comment on the inflexibility of the communicator.

- Rapport is meeting individuals in their model of the world.

- People are doing the best they can, given the choices they believe are available to them.

- People will always make the best choice available to them at the time, but usually there are lots of other choices that they are not aware of.

- If what you are doing isn't working, do something different.

- If you always do what you've always done, you'll always get what you've always got.

- Individuals with the most flexibility have the highest probability of achieving the responses they desire.

- It is easier to change yourself than others.

- To change somebody else, first change yourself.

- Change can be quick and lasting.

The Basic Skills for Problem-Solving with NLP

One cannot be an effective rider until one feels clearly and can discern the communications of his horse.

CHARLES DE KUNFFY *Training Strategies for Dressage Riders*

CHAPTER 1

Working from the Inside

Beyond the necessary physical skills, which constitute the sport in riding, we need
to address the rider's mind, that is, the science of riding, and the rider's spirit.
CHARLES DE KUNFFY *The Ethics and Passions of Dressage*

As you see it right now, your body is the physical
picture, in 3D, of what you are thinking.
DEEPAK CHOPRA *Quantum Healing*

Why do we, as riders, need to be aware of what is going on in our minds? Not just so that we can use our minds to improve what our bodies do, but because our minds *already* influence our bodies. We are, and do, what we think. This chapter summarises what we know about the body-mind connection, and so lays the foundation for the rest of the book. It has three sections. The first sets out some key points about the mind-body relationship as we understand it today, together with their implications for riders. The second looks more specifically at how each of us structures our experience – in other words, how we actually do what we call 'thinking'. The third explains how we give meaning to our experience according to its relative level of importance and the implications this has when we are trying to make changes.

The Mind-Body Connection

Riding is such a subtle form of communication, and as we progress we are always trying to refine it further: we strive to make our aiding more and more unobtrusive, more elegant; we aim to respond more and more quickly to the information the horse gives us in his behaviour; in training we ask him for more rapidity, subtlety and surety in his responses. This applies in all disciplines. The highest compliment we can be paid by an observer is that we 'don't seem to be doing anything'. Podhajsky, for example, talks of how an advanced dressage horse will respond to a slight shifting of the rider's weight from one side of the stirrup to the other. In terms of our ideal, an aid we can see is too gross.

Good riders in any discipline know, of course, how much precise physical control is needed to achieve such fine communication. There are no shortcuts, since muscles take time to develop and to train. But what of the accidental, unintended, habitual messages that we also give – messages which may be the unthought-of result of life-experience, such as lopsidedness, or of specific past events, such as accidents, traumas or injuries; or, most treacherous of all, of emotions? Anxiety, fear, lack of confidence, doubt, trying too hard. Most of us know that these have affected us at one time or another. Our bodies act them out too. And our horses, sensitive as they are, receive and respond to these unintended messages too.

This book is about riding, and especially dressage, as acts of communication – best of all, of mutual communication. If we are to communicate in the clearest, most effective way we can, we need to become more fully aware of how we do it, so that we can 'clean up' what we do that doesn't work or that gets in the way of our intended messages, and do more of what we do that is clear and effective. We also need to notice and be able to interpret accurately what our horses are 'saying' to us by their behaviour.

So, how does the mind-body connection work? Once upon a time, people thought of mind and body as separate – the Anglo-Saxons talked of the body as the 'bone-house' of the mind. Once science began to help us understand how the body was made and worked, there seemed to be more difficulty in identifying what, if anything, could be separated out from physical structure and events. While we talk of 'mind', 'brain', 'feelings', or 'thoughts' we now have enough information to know that these are not *things* or even *events* but ongoing *processes*. This understanding allows us to consider some important issues.

Mind and body are aspects of the same thing

We now know that our bodies cannot help but act out what we are used to calling 'thought' and 'feeling', because mind and body are a complex set of interconnected systems. This works two ways, of course: we can deliberately make use of this, so that in thinking in a certain way (for example, making a picture of what we intend) we give our body the best chance of achieving it; we also have to recognise that what we think and feel, our body will inevitably be communicating physically. *What we think, or feel, our body does.*

For example, you might meet a friend and immediately say: 'You look worried: are you all right?' It took you only seconds to observe and evaluate a whole range of information to reach this conclusion. Your friend probably did not intend to look worried: it 'just happened'. In relation to riding, I described earlier how my anxiety about cantering used to lead to physical tension, which was then passed on to my horse.

- Think of an example from your experience when what you felt or thought had an unwanted effect.

- Think of an example when a thought or feeling had a beneficial effect.

States and reactions

Thoughts and feelings are expressed by the body in two ways:

1. Regular, habitual patterns (states)

2. Reactions to specific events or circumstances.

1. States

A state is a complex collection of mind-body events which relates to a particular situation, role or experience. A state will include things like your focus of attention (broad, specific, shifting or steady), your posture and movement, and your beliefs, feelings and mental processing. If you teach, you may have a special 'teaching state'. Since you have been through various formal educational institutions, you probably also have a 'pupil state'. You may have states connected with work, leisure, partnering, parenting, being on holiday and so on. Within riding, you may have states relating to schooling, hacking and competing. States can also become part of our very identity, and result in automatic, habitual physical patterns. The common phrase 'a stiff upper lip' shows this clearly. When we are about to cry, the upper lip begins to tremble. If we want or need to hide this from others, we try to tense, or stiffen, the muscles in the upper lip. This may happen in a few circumstances only; it may happen more extensively, as for example when it was thought unmanly to cry; or it may become a way of life, as among soldiers; or even a feature of the whole British culture. What started out

as a simple mind-body experience has by that stage become very far-reaching –
but it is still one in which body and mind are both involved.

> Let's look at another example. If I am schooling, my mind is on what I intend
> to do and how we are doing it. My awareness is largely trained on physical
> experience (which NLP calls **kinesthetic**) – and is narrow in focus. The day's
> events are automatically banished as soon as I get on my horse. I am calm,
> because I see my role as one of teaching or enabling. I am thinking about
> giving clear signals and monitoring the responses I get. I am constantly
> evaluating. If I am hacking, in contrast, I am not 'on duty'. Therefore, I am not
> evaluating the communication process so intently. I have a broader focus – I
> enjoy looking out at the countryside, watching out for wildlife, noticing trees
> and flowers. My conversation with the horse is less intensely kinesthetic, and
> more auditory – I talk to him or often sing to him. My emotional range is
> greater. I may be excited by a brisk canter over an open field, relaxed as we
> potter along, or anxious about traffic on the main road.

The following exercises ask you about your own states. You may find it helpful to
jot down your answers, so that you have details at hand for later exercises.

- Take two different situations, at least one of which involves you and your
  horse, and compare your states in each.

- Which of your states are specially helpful?

- Are there any states that you would like to change in any way?

2. Responses to specific circumstances

It is obvious that we respond to here-and-now situations with here-and-now
reactions. Something goes well: we are pleased, relax or feel joyful. However, it
doesn't stop there. Our delight or relaxation is as much a set of bodily changes as
a changed awareness. So it is also communicated instantaneously to our horse. It
is not surprising if we then get a chain or cascade reaction:

Success ► *good feelings* ► *bodily change* ► *relaxed communication* ►
better rapport ► *better work*

might be one such chain.

On the other hand:

> *Straight centre line to halt* ▶ *relief* ▶ *rider relaxes* ▶ *rider's legs relax* ▶ *horse moves in final halt*

is another chain with apparently the same sequence but less desirable results!

As these examples show, a response is not self-contained: it has consequences. An evasion by the horse may make the rider disappointed, irritated or cross: these emotions transfer through the rider's body-language back to the horse, resulting perhaps in increased resistance, anxiety or a loss of sparkle and forwardness. The rider then reacts to the horse's response, and so on… Another chain is created. Another example is the way horses and riders can 'wind each other up' in competitions, which we will look at later in the book.

But events do not occur in a vacuum. For example, a horse may be frightened or distracted when being schooled or in competition; the rider copes at the time; but the rider's response, both to the event itself and to the horse's immediate reaction to it, is coloured by the rider's own personal history. We are learning creatures: we use our past experience to manage the present and predict the future. We also generalise from experiences which have been important for us. Someone whose past experience has taught them *'I'll cope'* or *'I can think on my feet'* or *'Never mind, just try again'* will find it easier to deal with a spook in the middle of a test than someone who has learnt to think *'I'll be all right provided nothing goes wrong'* or *'Just my luck: things never go right for me'* or *'How come I'm the one who always gets the raw deal?'*

These statements are ones of belief about the world and one's place in it. You might find it helpful to list some of your everyday beliefs and their possible consequences.

Memory is not a factual recording

NLP helps us to recognise that memory is simply our own way of storing our individual experience.

To the best of our scientific and clinical knowledge, the brain stores information about everything that happens to us (provided that we register the information at the time, consciously or unconsciously). Of course, this does not mean that we can recall all past events at will, because some information is encoded unconsciously. Information is stored in clusters, linked by associations or similarities. The same event would be stored differently by different people, because it had different meanings for them or because everyone's brains work slightly differently.

Some riders, for example, love riding stallions: others fear them. The 'same' events involving stallions could be stored very differently. Someone who fears them may store a good performance as an exception, whereas someone who loves their strength and exuberance may think of it as just typical. One rider will store information primarily through bodily (kinesthetic) awareness, another mainly through pictures.

Whereas an unedited tape or video recording replays the actual events, human (and probably also equine) memory is always edited! Mental processes are far too fast, and many of them too far out of awareness, for us to be able to monitor them accurately and fully as they happen. Since experience is registered by the body-mind as a whole, any memory will be stored in relation not just to the circumstances of the event but as also to the state which was characteristic of or evoked it. Researchers in neurobiology (the science of the body-mind) call this **state-dependent memory**. It works two ways: whenever the memory is activated, so is the state; and whenever the state is activated, so is the memory.

Let's look at an example.

Karen tended to look down most of the time. She knew she should look ahead, and her teacher kept reminding her. Nonetheless, when she was not thinking about her posture, her head returned to this bent position. When I asked her to pay attention to the state which went with this head posture, she said she felt anxiety, a 'weight on her shoulders', a wish to be invisible. She remembered feeling like this as a child. I asked her to straighten up, and pay attention to the state which went along with that very different posture. She said it was one of confidence, of knowing that friends and family believed in her and wanted her to succeed. When asked to imagine riding like this, she felt increased enjoyment and confidence. Both feelings were strongest at the base of her neck. Knowing this, we were then able to build a way of her 'anchoring' the feelings of confidence and their associated posture so that they became automatic for her – and not just when she was riding.

- Think about something you really enjoy. Notice the state that evokes in you. As you pay attention to the details, you will probably find that you remember more, and that the state itself becomes more marked.

- Think of an activity or occasion you mildly dislike or that makes you slightly tense. What changes in state do you notice?

■ Go back to the first situation again. Is there any feature of that situation or that state that would help you in the second? It might be a different thought, a different way of processing the information – for example, pictures rather than body feelings, or vice versa, or perhaps a different body posture. Notice what this key difference is, and keep it in mind while you slowly return to the less pleasant situation, so that by adding in the extra, more pleasant, feature you can change it and improve how you feel about it.

Horses have state-dependent memories, too, as the earlier example of the schoolmaster who wouldn't be bridled showed. While we still don't know what experiences may have triggered this anxiety state, he clearly learnt at some time that having his head handled could be dangerous or painful. On the other hand, our younger horse, Vals, who was imported from Russia as a newly-broken but unschooled four-year-old, was from the beginning very calm in traffic and with noise. We know that he was bred and reared at a large stud-farm and then spent six months with about a hundred other horses in barns near Moscow airport before being exported, so it seems likely that his calmness is the result of learning then that activity and loud noises were not dangerous to him.

■ Does your horse seem to have any state-dependent memories?

States may be triggered accidentally or deliberately

When we trigger a state, we reinforce it. Good teaching and learning, of course, rests on this principle, and may in fact build up a routine or sequence of behaviours in order to help us learn.

Like many riders, in our yard we begin schooling sessions by walking on a loose rein. Obviously, this helps horses to warm up and begin to work their muscles. This is like athletes limbering up before a training session. It also allows them to begin to soften and use their backs, preventing injury and promoting correct, supple, work.

The walking also helps to set up a schooling state. Entering the sand school, mounting, walking around, make a sequence which both rider and horse know will lead to schooling. The walking is calm, measured, unhurried, just as the session itself is intended to be.

Karen and Billy

'A weight on her shoulders'.

A state of confidence, knowing that friends and family believed in her.

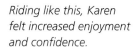 *Riding like this, Karen felt increased enjoyment and confidence.*

Our first horse, Tristan, was trained and spent much of his working life as a lunge-schoolmaster. He loved being lunged. He even enjoyed the horse-walker, and objected to having to work in the school while other horses were being exercised in the walker. One wet day when my daughter couldn't find a lunge rope she discovered that, if she stood in the middle of the school, Tristan would lunge himself around her on voice command alone! For him, the combination of being in the school and having a person in the middle was sufficient to activate a lunge-state which he enjoyed.

■ Do you have a routine for starting a schooling session? How does it help you and your horse establish a good state for learning? What other routines do you have, and how do they contribute to useful states?

Muscles have memories

This was a phrase one of my tutors used when I was training to become a psychotherapist. I used to be rather sceptical about it, but after years of clinical experience and reading about the workings of the body-mind I now believe it to be true.

I believe that it describes an important process which affects us all: a memory is not just an idea, or a 'recording' in the mind, as I have been trying to show. It is a state as well. Therefore, the state may be triggered, or recalled, when the body deliberately or accidentally repeats an experience in which it has learnt something.

A few years ago I had some Alexander lessons to help me correct my head position when riding. Years of short sight had led me to tip my head back to look through the lower part of my lenses where the prescription was at its strongest. This in itself is a muscle memory, since nowadays my eyes change only infrequently, and my glasses give me good vision. My Alexander teacher asked me one day to 'let my weight sink down through my ankles', and I realised that I was blocking this from happening in my left ankle. Then I remembered that I had once broken that ankle – but that was over thirty years ago! Exploring this further, I realised that this was also one reason why I found it difficult to let my ankles absorb movement when riding and why I had difficulty in developing a soft and following seat. My muscles had remembered without fail for over thirty years, long after the ankle injury had healed. In computer terms, time for the programme to be updated!

Working with Karen on one occasion, I helped her explore a body memory problem: her toes kept creeping down. When she got in touch with the body experience, she remembered how, for years, she used to wear very high heels to work, and would walk around the house on tiptoe even after she had come home and taken her shoes off. We looked for a different muscle memory that would help her make the change. It had to be one which also involved her feet. Fortunately, we have all walked in flat shoes, or without shoes, at some time. When I asked her about this, she remembered pestering her mother for a special pair of red shoes when she was little, and how proud she had been of them. She had kept on glancing down to admire them, and lifting her toes to see them more easily. Because this was such a good memory, she was easily able to install her new programme, and just reminding herself about the red shoes from time to time has been enough to help her make the better pattern into a habit.

ABOVE *Body memory: blocking with the left ankle.*

Reminding herself about the red shoes.

■ Do you have any muscle memories that either help or hinder your riding? If they hinder it, can you find some alternative muscle memories to put in their place?

The mind does not store actual experience

What the mind stores is not experience itself, but a translation, symbol or representation of that experience.

Experience happens to us – and in us! When we store it in the mind, we register not the event itself, but the details that mean something to us. Some of these will be muscle memories or states; some might be what we learnt from the experience; some will be in picture, sound or kinesthetic form. None of these *is* the actual experience: instead, it's a symbolisation or representation of it in the terms in which the mind works. Because of this, we can make use of other symbolisations or representations to change it. The example of the red shoes shows us one way this can happen. The red shoes had a powerful meaning of pleasure, pride and success, a strong colour, and a set of body memories, so they could act as a symbol to help bring about the changes the rider wanted.

Pictures, words, sounds can all 'stand for' mental events or sequences in this way. 'Swing to the trot' calls up our experience of swinging, particularly its rhythm and ease. We hear the word, the mind searches for its meaning, and re-translates the relevant aspect of the meaning into rhythmical body movement. But because we are different from each other, any symbol may work well for some people, less well for others. Since every symbol is a translation, the flavour of the original is partially lost: as with translating from one language to another, it is at best the nearest approximation. If we have to work too hard at 'getting' a symbol, it won't help us so much as one which really suits us well.

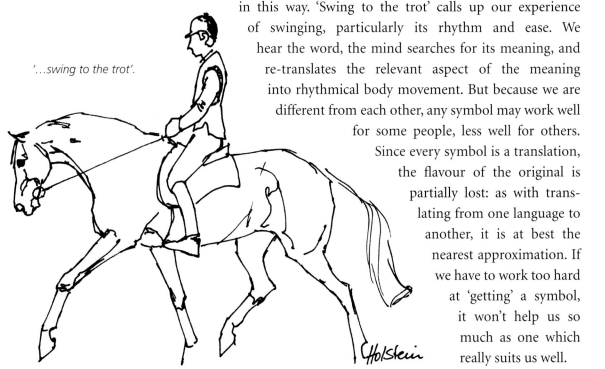

'…swing to the trot'.

Holstein

■ Think of some ideas or symbols that help you in your riding. Note them down. What is it about them that you have found connects with you most strongly?

Learning is stored in a context

Because learning (which is an aspect of memory) is stored in relation to the original experience, it is stored in a particular 'frame' of context or meaning.

It is hardly too strong to say that events mean what we believe them to mean. In other words, it is the labels we give to experience which make all the difference. This is because the label is our understanding of what the experience means to us, and this determines how we respond to it.

Event ► reaction ► label(meaning) ► learning ► expectations/beliefs/values

A good example is how we label the following state:

faster heartbeat and breathing; adrenalin in the system; feeling hyped up; faster movements and reactions; attentiveness.

It describes fear, doesn't it? Yes. It describes excitement? Yes, again. Mostly, in deciding which label to give, we are guided by the context. Was it the sort of thing which was likely to cause fear (i.e. unpleasant, made us want to be somewhere else, run away etc.)? Or was it stimulating, fun, interesting, new, pleasantly unexpected, likely to cause excitement? In this case, the body often doesn't have a way to decide for us. And even if we agree it's excitement, some people love being excited but others people prefer to be calm. So excitement isn't automatically a pleasant state to be in.

The label 'fear' or 'excitement' is how we **frame** the experience. As with framing a picture, how we frame an experience can make all the difference to how we understand it. If we frame a testing ride as 'a challenge' we will not feel the same as we do when we frame it as 'an achievement' or 'an opportunity'. As the chapter on competition shows, some people regularly under-perform because they frame dressage tests as 'being judged', with all the associations that has, where others may frame them as 'a chance to show what my horse can do', or 'giving him some ring experience', both of which have different associations and lead to different feelings.

- Think about having a lesson with your trainer. How do you frame being a pupil?

- Think about schooling your horse. How do you frame acting as his trainer yourself?

If you wish to change how you frame these or other roles, you can explore other ways of framing the same information. A *task*, a *chore* and a *challenge* both describe something which has to be done, but the implications are very different. Discover what happens if you take one of your 'tasks' or 'chores' and think of it as a 'challenge' – or the other way around. You can be sure that the meaning will alter. If you find that it alters for the better, and you feel better about it as a result, you have changed and enriched your experience. Even if you prefer, having once tried it out, to continue to think of it as you did at first, you will know that you now have more options.

- Think of some other things which have related meanings in this way, and find out how reframing can change how you feel about them.

The mind works both consciously and unconsciously

The thoughts that go though our heads, like the words on the screen of a computer, are ones of which we are **conscious**. The mind does a lot of other work, outside our awareness, and this processing we call **unconscious**. Much of memory, for example, is unconscious. I am writing these words on a word-processor: what you and I can see is what appears on the screen, but that is the result of processes which are going on elsewhere, out of sight. A similar relationship exists between conscious and unconscious activity in the mind.

When we learn a skill, we do so consciously, whether the skill is physical, social or intellectual. We are aware of noticing, memorising, repeating, refining the skill. After a while, as we become more familiar with it, we become less aware of the skill itself, and more aware of what we are using it for. Reading is one good example: driving a car, or riding a horse, are others. When we first learnt to read, we first had to learn that black marks on paper meant something, that they meant different things, that they represented sounds, that sounds represented things and processes and could be combined together to make meanings. Now you are just reading for meaning alone. When we first rode a horse, we found it difficult to be aware of so much at one time: it never seemed possible that we would get it all together. Now the basic skills are automatic, and we are concerned with much subtler detail. Not how to stay on, or steer, but how to shape a half-pass, how to tell if the quarters are engaged and if not how to engage them, how to judge the take-off point for a fence, or estimate the speed to cover a certain distance. The basic skills have passed from conscious into unconscious storage.

There is a very useful model of skill learning which can help us understand how this happens.

1. To start with, we don't even know what it is we don't know (for example, beginning riders don't know shoulder-in exists). This stage is called one of **unconscious incompetence**.

2. Next, we may become aware that there is such a thing as shoulder-in, and what it involves. But we can't do it yet. This is the stage of **conscious incompetence**.

3. We might then set out to learn shoulder-in, and even become quite proficient at it, trying hard to get it right. This is the stage of **conscious competence**.

4. Finally, we reach the point of such familiarity with the movement and all it involves that we cease to be concerned with it as such, and might be thinking instead about how to weave it into a sequence, or deepening the angle, or maintaining the impulsion, or using it to engage the inside hind. This is the stage of **unconscious competence**.

1. *Unconscious incompetence:*
   'What are they doing?'

2. *Conscious incompetence:*
   'I can't do that.'

3. *Competence: 'I can do that.'*

4. *Unconscious competence:*
   Rider says to himself 'Fair angle,
   but I'm leaning forward rather.'

This model is useful for riders, because knowing which stage we are at helps us explore appropriate ways of progressing through the stages, using mental as well as physical exercises to do so. There are lots of different ideas for this throughout the book. It also helps us to remember that horses seem to have a similar sequence in their learning, as we can observe in their training. Like us, they may have to concentrate hard when being asked to learn a new movement (conscious incompetence), and can sometimes be seen 'showing off' a newly mastered movement even when it is not asked for (conscious competence). Once they can do it easily, the movement flows simply in response to the aid (unconscious competence).

Every time we add something to our learning, this process repeats. And because of the mind-body connection, our bodies and those of our horses tend to mirror the different stages. Conscious incompetence may involve anxiety and tension (many young horses tense and hollow through transitions, and more advanced ones will show similar reactions when asked for changes or pirouettes). Conscious competence may sometimes appear correct but wooden, or without sparkle. Unconscious competence, the goal that we work towards, flows with energy and brilliance, or with quiet ease.

There is a saying in Papua-New Guinea which one of my NLP teachers shared with us: *Until it's in the muscles, it's only a rumour.* One of the intentions of this book is to offer you mental strategies to help you get your learning into your muscles – and those of your horse.

The effect of emotion

Since emotion conveys muscle messages, it may confuse, or conflict with, the horse's training and performance.

We all know how sensitive horses are, and how observant. As prey animals, their safety depended upon rapid reactions. One of the commonest problems riders experience – especially in competition – is that of conveying their anxiety to their horses. Since emotions and thoughts involve changes in chemical and electrical signals, and translate instantaneously into body states and behaviour, they will be immediately available to the horse as information. Since we are the horse's herd leader, he is likely to follow our lead. Fine, if we are calm and concentrated: less so if we are anxious, fearful or distracted. As a judge, I am sometimes aware that horses I have seen working excellently in training under-perform in the arena. It seems likely that they are being affected not just by the distractions which are present at a show but also by their rider's feelings and beliefs. But even in schooling or hacking, our emotions can get in the way. Many of the strategies explored in this book can help us to deal with these confusing or conflicting messages, so that our conversations with the horse become clearer, simpler and more effective.

Representational Systems

When we think, we use information about the world which has come to us through our five senses: seeing, hearing, feeling, smelling and tasting. NLP refers to these ways of processing as **Visual (V)**, **Auditory (A)**, **Kinesthetic (K)**, **Olfactory (O)** and **Gustatory (G)**. 'Gustatory' is not a very commonly used word: it comes from the Latin word *gustare*, to taste, and means 'concerned with tasting or the sense of taste', so it properly describes any physical or mental processes which relate to that fifth sense.

All of us use all of the representational systems to some extent, but we have our favourites.

> ▪ Take a moment to write down a description of something very familiar to you – for example, the way to work – or something special – for example, what kind of holiday you most enjoy, or what you really like about your horse. Then look at the words you have used. You are likely to find that some of them are metaphoric, indicating which kinds of sensory experience are most important to you.

Here are some examples.

If you get on well with someone, do you:
see eye to eye with them
feel you are *on the same wavelength*
hold fast to the same beliefs?

- *Words and phrases that indicate **visual** processing include:* clear, bright, dull, fuzzy, blurred, point of view, perspective, see what you mean.

- *Words and phrases that indicate **auditory** processing include:* quiet, loud, sharp, scratchy, distinct, mellow, word for word, tune in, in tune, off-key.

- *Words and phrases that indicate **kinesthetic** processing include:* heavy, weighty, light, burdensome, oppressive, small, large, knotty, slippery, get to grips with, grasp, hold on to, a feel for something.

- *Words and phrases that indicate **olfactory** processing include:* scent, smell, stench, aroma, smell a rat, a nose for something.

- *Words and phrases that indicate **gustatory** processing include:* sweet, sour, bland, flavour, bitter, taste, make you sick, sour to your stomach, a bad taste in the mouth.

Holstein

Horse and rider in passage.

*Rider A, watching, thinks: 'I bet that feels wonderful!' (**Kinesthetic**)*

*Rider B thinks: 'Just look at that!' (**Visual**)*

*Rider C thinks: 'Get that rhythm!' (**Auditory**)*

*Rider D thinks: 'The sweet smell of success!' (**Olfactory**)*

*Rider E thinks: 'He makes me sick with envy!' (**Gustatory**)*

The first three systems (Visual, Auditory, Kinesthetic) are more common favourites, and most riders will tend to favour either Visual or Kinesthetic or a mixture of both. It is important to remind ourselves that there is no better or worse in this: it is the outcome which is better or worse, not the process itself. Many dressage riders, for example, tend to keep watching their horse's neck to see whether he is on the bit or not. This tends to be reflected in a tendency to ride the horse from the front to the back – with too much reliance on the hands shaping the neck – rather than from back to front, with the seat and legs being used to increase the activity of the hind legs and ride the horse up from behind into the frame of the contact. In addition, as the rider looks down at the horse's neck, the rider's head will tend to droop forward, thus increasing the weight on the horse's shoulder and in effect encouraging him to go on the forehand.

However, when we are in touch with experience in a kinesthetic way, we also tend to look down – specifically, we tend to look down and to the right. A kinesthetically oriented rider, therefore, may also end up weighting the horse's shoulder because this rider, too, is looking down – although probably inclining the head down and defocusing the eyes rather than actually *looking at* the neck. I remember my trainer pointing out to me more than once that my head was angled forward and to the right as I 'got in touch' with my kinesthetic experience. What she actually said was 'All your marbles seem to have rolled into your right ear!'

If you look at the photograph of Charles de Kunffy on the cover of this book, you will see how very upright he is, and how he is looking straight ahead. He is connecting internally with the experience of riding his horse without this affecting how his body is orientated. While it is natural for our bodies to reflect the kind of processing we naturally favour, we may have to learn to override this in order to avoid giving unintended messages to our horse.

The Logical Levels

The NLP concept of Logical Levels is one which helps us to work out what kinds of experiences we are having and just what kind of importance they have for us. The Logical Levels are:

- **Identity**

- **Beliefs and Values**

- **Capability**

- **Behaviour**

- **Environment**

One way to remember the levels is to think of them as a hierarchy, with the most crucial and intimate level (identity) at the top, and the most peripheral (environment) at the bottom. We can also arrange them as a set of concentric circles, with identity in the middle and environment on the outside. Difficulties that we have can usually be dealt with much more effectively if we know the level or levels involved.

Issues which affect identity are, literally, closer to home, more crucial, more sensitive, more vulnerable. Issues of environment are less personally loaded for us. Each of the levels helps us to answer a particular question:

- **Identity** tells us **who**

- **Beliefs and Values** are about **why**

- **Capability** answers questions about **how**

- **Behaviour** tells us about **what**

- **Environment** covers questions about **where** and **when**

If we are aware of the level on which we are having a problem we can often find a solution on the same level. For example, if the horse barges out of the stable when the door is opened (behaviour), a firm 'No' and a touch, or even slap, on the shoulder may be needed every time the door is opened until he has 'got the message'.

Sometimes, though, identifying the level where the problem occurs may allow us to discover that it is actually coming from another level. For example, a rider may think she is a poor rider (capability or even identity) because her horse doesn't obey her (behaviour). Realising that there is a mismatch allows us to find out whether his behaviour results from the rider's inappropriate actions (her behaviour) or lack of skill or knowledge (capability), or perhaps beliefs (she thinks horses should be cajoled not told). Usually, finding that the issue is arising on a less serious level than identity makes us feel a lot better – and encourages us to keep looking for new strategies and solutions. We often feel more helpless to change identity issues, because we often think of identity as fixed like the colour of our eyes or the shape of our nose. (Actually, NLP also helps us to understand that identity is not a fixed thing but more of a set of familiar processes – and can therefore be modified.)

If we are attempting to correct ourselves, or others whom we are helping, it is always best done at the lowest level which is relevant. Not 'you are incompetent' (identity) but 'your attitude may be getting in the way here' (belief), or 'you need to learn how to deepen your seat more (capability)', or 'you need to turn your shoulders into the movement more' (behaviour), or 'try that canter strike off from the corner where he will be set up more easily for the bend' (environment).

On the other hand, praise is always most effective when given at an identity level, either as well as or instead of at other levels. Praise for us as a whole person spreads throughout the entire system!

- Take an example of some comments on your riding you have found helpful. On what level were these comments made? Was it the same level as the level of what was being commented upon?

- Take some comments (perhaps on a test sheet, or from your trainer) which you have found less helpful even though the content was accurate. Which logical levels were involved?

- Take a problem you have encountered in your riding. On what logical level did you experience it? On what level do you now think it originated?

- Take a success you have had with your riding. What logical levels were involved?

Jot your answers down. You may find it useful to return to these examples at other times in the book as you gain more strategies for working with them.

As riders, we are skilled athletes helping to develop the equine athletes whom we care for and who are our partners. Riding cannot happen without the conversations we have together. The more aware we become of our own body-mind processing, the more we can develop our skills to make these conversations clearer and more effective, and the more we can use that knowledge to develop effective internal and external strategies for dealing with the issues, needs and problems we come across with our horses.

We can also use this heightened awareness to discover more about how we do the things we do that are successful. Discovering what works, from within our own experience, strengthens our confidence and enables us to build our own recipes for success.

CHAPTER 2

Working from the Outside

Know the basic nature, the momentary mood, and the potential
anxieties of your horse while in his company.
CHARLES DE KUNFFY *Training Strategies for Dressage Riders*

Children notice. We can regain the curiosity and acuity we had as children.
IAN MCDERMOTT AND JOSEPH O'CONNOR *Principles of NLP*

In the previous chapter I explained some NLP concepts which can offer us
some of the elements of a 'brain user's owner-driver manual'. In this chapter
I'm going to focus on a range of NLP concepts and skills which can help us
work from the outside. These are **Calibration**, **Contrastive Analysis**, **Loops** and
Modelling. Essentially, these are skills of observation, which help us improve
our ability to gather accurate and detailed information, and offer us ways to use
that information more effectively to improve what we do and to bring about the
changes we want.

Calibration

Calibration is the skill of measuring small changes. People who are good at any
physical skill are good at calibration; so are those who are skilled with people.
But so are we all, in some ways, even though we may not know that calibrating is
what we are doing. When we wake up in the morning and have a feeling that we
are in some way off-colour, we have been calibrating, perhaps unconsciously,
differences from the way we usually feel, and on that basis have reached the
conclusion that something isn't right. It may be several hours, or even days,

before those slight differences have grown into something we can label as a cold, or flu, or depression, or a pulled muscle. When you are having a lesson, you may be amazed sometimes at how your teacher can pinpoint where a problem stems from, and what you need to do to correct it. The everyday word 'pinpoint' tells us how small such a piece of important information can be.

Good teachers, good trainers, in whatever sphere, are good calibrators. They notice small changes in detail, and how they relate to the overall pattern of what they are looking at. That is another way to describe calibration: it's a bit like those 'spot the difference' pairs of pictures in children's puzzle books. But whereas in that case both examples are available at once, with calibration one example is in the memory. The remembered example may be from a few minutes – or even seconds – ago, last week or last year. As we get better at the skill, we get better at monitoring changes from moment to moment – and this gives us the ability to recognise the situation we are working with and to make desired changes very quickly. Sometimes my trainer has said that, for example, a shoulder-in or half-pass began well but then fell apart after a few strides: 'It would have been better to abandon it as soon as it started to go wrong rather than continuing', she might say. But often, her speed at calibration was faster than mine, so whereas she could have made an earlier decision to abandon the attempt, I couldn't. Nowadays, I am often faster than I was – but usually still not fast enough to make a correction before she comments: 'He's losing impulsion!' 'I know!' 'Well…' ('do something about it, then…' is implied).

If we want to improve our ability to calibrate, it helps to concentrate on one thing at a time, otherwise we get overwhelmed with information and find it hard to sort out. The dreaded neck-watching is something most dressage riders are reasonably good at calibrating: we know some of the key features of how a neck should be – rounded, soft muscles, bulge near the crest, triangular bulge in front of the saddle. We watch, often to the detriment of true 'throughness' from behind, for the small changes that tell us our horse is on or off the bit or going from one to the other.

If we have the chance of watching other riders, we have a freer attention to practice our calibration. Again, it's best to pick one feature and really watch for that. What does a 'swinging back' look like? What tells us that the horse is 'engaging behind' – or not? We can learn from books, videos and experts what we should be looking for, and this will help us to 'get our eye in'. Once we know what we are looking for, we can begin to watch how, moment by moment, a working horse and rider get closer to this ideal, or further away from it.

If you have the opportunity of writing for dressage judges, this can also be a good way of learning, since they have to comment very rapidly on what they are

In both pictures Karen and Billy are working correctly in trot, yet the overall impression is quite different. The top image is calm, soft, effortless yet perhaps lacking tone.

The lower picture, taken later in the same schooling session, shows more effort – a 'trying' state. We can all recognise the difference at a glance, but what are the specific differences that make up the overall difference? How many can you see?

seeing. Watching good teaching and training is even better, because good trainers give their pupils ongoing feedback on small details as they notice them, and suggest small improvements they can make. So, as observers, we are also being taught. If you are able to have your own riding recorded on video, even if there is no teacher present, you can later stop and start and pause and compare details of what you see, always being mindful of small changes and small detail.

So far, I have talked about visual calibration. But we can do it with our other senses, too. When you ride, you probably think from time to time: 'he's going well today', or 'that felt stiff', or 'I'm bouncing too much'. Ask yourself, if you can spare a moment or two more, '*What tells me* he's going well? *How* is that particularly different today? (or from a few moments ago)?' Ask '*Where* do I feel the stiffness? *What is different* from when he feels softer?' 'When I bounce, *what things am I noticing that are different* from when I don't bounce – or bounce less? Is *he* different (more lively, or more stiff) – or is it *me*? If it's me, *where* is the lack of flexibility? Is it physical – if so, in which bit of my body? Or is it mental – Friday night, a hard week and I'm tired, perhaps I'm anxious because I find this movement difficult and so my anxiety is affecting the basics of how I'm riding.'

This may seem like a lot to do – but it takes up far longer as words on a page than as thought in our heads. And like all skills, the more we do it the easier it gets – it passes from conscious incompetence ('Gosh, I never even thought to ask that question') to conscious competence ('Now what is going on here?') to unconscious competence, where we simply make the necessary adjustments after rapid, automatic monitoring.

Here are some areas to home in on: changes in 'feel'; 'through' or 'not through'; engaged or not engaged; swinging or not swinging; on the bit/not on the bit – but without looking down!; soft or not soft; impulsive or inactive; stepping under or not; straight or not straight.

To begin with, it is easier to work from the extremes. If you have a trainer or knowledgeable friend who can watch you, get them to tell you when your horse is 'through' or 'hollow', for example. Notice and memorise the feeling. As you get more confident that you can recognise the extremes, then try telling your helper when you think your horse is 'through' or 'hollow'. That way, you will get feedback on how accurate you are. The more you pay attention, the faster you'll get at calibrating smaller differences, until eventually you'll be effortlessly processing the information. Then you will be in a position to work with that information to the fullest extent of your skills – and in fact it will be easier, because you will only have smaller corrections to make.

It seems fairly obvious that we can develop our skills as rider-trainers through improving visual and kinesthetic observation. But there is another sense we need to remember, too – hearing. A friend of mine once knew a blind trainer: she had developed her hearing so greatly that she was able to monitor what a horse was doing and how he was going through hearing alone. Even more astounding, she could work with one horse in an arena in which several others were also working – and sort them all out from each other by sound alone. While this is an exceptional example, we can all learn from it.

- As you watch a horse working, shut your eyes and listen for a while. What can you hear? Differences in gait, probably fairly easily. Ask yourself if the horse is working in a consistent rhythm. Probably not difficult. How would you be able to tell from sound alone if he was active or inactive? Could you tune into crispness or dragging sounds that would help? How might you tell if his strides were suspended or not? When you think you know, open your eyes and check. Unlike the blind trainer, you have another way of verifying your impression.

- Practice asking the same questions when you are actually on your horse. Get a good rhythmical trot, then listen to it. Find a forward swinging canter, and listen to it. If you are in a school on your own, be bold and shut your eyes – there is nowhere much he can go! Allow your horse to slop along and lose impulsion in walk, or hurry him up until he's beginning to lose rhythm, and listen to how the sound of his footfalls changes. Is he dragging or lifting his feet? Is the proper beat (the 'purity of the gait') becoming compromised? Is he 'uphill' and light, or 'downhill' and thudding? If you have the opportunity of being lunged, you can also do this shut-eye work then.

Contrastive Analysis

When we calibrate, we are noticing primarily how things are changing. When we compare things which are strongly different, or involve a number of factors, we are making what NLP calls a contrastive analysis. We are looking to find all the ways in which one example differs from the other.

- Write down all the features you can think of that make for a good riding lesson. On another piece of paper, write down all the features of a bad lesson. Now compare the two. Some things may appear on both lists, positively on one and negatively on the other (For example, 'encourages me' versus 'discourages me'.) Some things may only appear on one list, which is fine.

- Now, on another piece of paper make two parallel columns. Put the things which appear on both lists on the same level as each other. Put the things which only occur on one list at the end – but ask yourself as you do if there should be an opposite which just did not occur to you, or if there really isn't one. If there is an opposite, now you come to think of it, fill it in.

- Now look at all the differences, and ask yourself which is the single most important one, in your view. For you, this will be what NLP calls the **difference that makes the difference**. That means it is the factor which has most impact on your experience – and therefore it largely determines how you feel about the situation and how you judge it. Other people may select other factors, because for them other things are most significant. But if we want to change something, it's the difference that makes the difference for *us* that is the key.

We can use contrastive analysis to help us understand something pretty general, like what it means to have a good lesson; something specific, like what makes a good or bad halt; something complex, like what distinguishes being in self-carriage as opposed to being on the forehand, or like the difference between submission and resistance. Sometimes people will broadly agree on what is the difference that makes a difference, and sometimes it will be more a matter of individual opinion. Contrastive analysis is a tool for sharpening our awareness of the different factors involved, and for distinguishing between them so as to find which is most significant.

When we find the difference that makes the difference, we have found where changes need to be made, or where we should resist any compromise. For example, some people may find learning easy if they are told what to do. For them, a good teacher is one who tells them clearly exactly what is needed. Other learners will want a teacher who explains why, not just what – and if that is the significant difference for them, they will need to bear it in mind if they ever have to change trainers. Even an excellent trainer of the other kind will not suit them so well, and so their learning will suffer. As with so much in NLP, there is no one right or wrong: we are all different, and the issue is 'what works'.

This has wider implications, too. If we are serious about our riding, we will be building up a range of ideas about what is 'good'; but it's important to remember that 'good', too, is relative. We cannot all have outstandingly talented, elastic horses; but we can use our skills to help the horses that we do have become more balanced, supple and obedient. In NLP terms, this is a **well-formed outcome** (goal) because, as I shall explain in more detail later, this goal – that each horse goes as well as he individually can – is actually achievable. There is more on how to formulate well-formed outcomes in Chapter Four.

When you have identified the difference that makes a difference for you, ask yourself whether it is within your power to change it or to maintain it. If not, you may need to alter or redefine something. A horse's conformation, for example, may make it difficult or impossible for him to do something well, or even at all, and if doing these exact things is the difference that makes the difference between happiness or frustration for you both, you have clarified a point of choice: you can keep him, and do more of what he can do; or find a horse more suited to what you have set your heart on. Contrastive analysis, and the identification of key differences, give us more power to manage the situations in which we find ourselves.

Loops

Often, in both our riding and non-riding lives, we find ourselves in a situation that repeats. It's like a piece of stuck dialogue. Family arguments, disagreements at work, battles with our horses can all get habitual. NLP calls these repeating patterns of interaction 'loops', because what happens goes round and round again. Somebody does or says something: the other person (or horse) reacts in a certain way; the first person then reacts to that reaction...and so on. Loops occur in 'good' situations as well as frustrating ones – but mostly we don't pay much attention to those! However, it is also worth looking at enabling loops because we can get useful information from them about what we do right, and then we can do it more.

> Here is an example of looping. Our younger horse, Vals, used to get excited about being turned out, and wouldn't wait for his headcollar to be taken off: as soon as he got to the field gate he would bound off, dragging the lead-rope through the hands of whoever was in charge and then charging round, bucking with excitement and enthusiasm. Then they would have to catch him to take the headcollar off. Where did the sequence begin? Perhaps with having his headcollar and turnout rug put on – these were signals of what was going to happen. Maybe the pattern began when he was young in Russia, with experiences we know nothing about. Certainly, he would get excited as he was led from the yard towards the field.

Vals used to get excited about being turned out… Vals and 007.

The next stage in the loop came from the human side: anticipating that he would be difficult, various people tried leading him down in a bridle, then in a Chifney. He managed to break both. The loop was now going like this:

RIDER – signals in some way that Vals is going to be turned out
VALS – excitement and anticipation
RIDER – restraint
VALS – breaks away anyway
RIDER – bruises, rope burns, anger, anxiety
VALS – anticipates that turnout time is now even more stressful

Like everyone else, I became bothered about turning him out. It was the one area of his life where he was at all 'difficult' – in fact this may have been part of the problem. He is a very person-centred horse, he wants to please, and when ridden he is never naughty or really exuberant – no bucks, few shies. It was almost as if the field was the one place where he felt he could really let himself go – and so he just couldn't wait.

How could I break the loop? Being cowardly – or ingenious – I decided that I had to get him to *want* to wait at the gate, and to achieve that I would have to give him an incentive and a distraction that would give us a few peaceful moments to take the headcollar off. I decided to give him an apple – but only when he was standing quietly inside the gate. I showed him the apple when I put his headcollar on in the box, and several times said 'wait' as he walked alongside me either jogging in anticipation of going out or turning his head towards the apple. Then I said 'wait' again once we got inside the gate, and then 'good boy' as he stood still. Then he got the apple. While he was eating it, off came the headcollar. He quickly learnt that the apple was coming, and the pattern changed. We now had another loop:

RIDER –   signals that it's time for turnout, shows V the apple
VALS –   walks calmly to field
RIDER –   says 'wait', if necessary
VALS –   stands at field gate
RIDER –   says 'good boy' or 'thank you', gives apple, removes headcollar
VALS –   charges off. After a while, he ceased to charge off, and walked instead.

After some time, the new loop seemed thoroughly established, and we stopped giving the apple, though we continued to say 'wait' and 'good boy'.

This worked fine all through the summer, but when winter came again and the horses were not going out every day, the old excitement started creeping back. Time to reinforce the loop we wanted again with a few apples!

As this example shows, looping is something which is part of every ongoing relationship. In itself, it is neither good nor bad. The trick is to identify the sequence, and, if the loop is a limiting, frustrating or ineffective one, to change the pattern. There are more examples in Chapter Eight. Riders and their horses get into loops in all areas of their lives together: in the stable, in the field, in training and in performance.

Think about looping patterns in your relationship with your horse. Can you think of some 'good' loops as well as some 'bad' ones? Try writing them out as a dialogue, which as much detail of behaviour, thought and feeling as you can. If the loop is a useful one, could you use any of its successful elements in other areas of your relationship with your horse? If the loop is a limiting one, can you find a place to change the sequence?

We also have loops within ourselves, which may involve both our thinking and our behaviour. For example:

RIDER – asks horse to do something

HORSE – doesn't obey

RIDER – thinks – I'm not good enough – whenever I try this it all goes wrong – I'm never going to do well in competition ▶ feels depressed ▶ schooling session goes downhill because rider becomes more tentative and more absorbed in own feelings, so less attentive to the horse.

After the initial resistance by the horse, this sequence was all within the rider. Some of it was made up of self-talk, which NLP calls **Internal Dialogue**, and which is an important, if often largely unrecognised, part of our thinking. Internal loops also often involve other types of internal representation – picturing, both remembered from the past and constructing images of the future; hearing (things people said, or might say), and the internal experiencing of physical and emotional events. Once we know the characteristic ways in which we construct our loops, we are in a position to change them. For example, when some riders think of trying something new, or of competing, they may make pictures of disaster scenarios, which then make them feel anxious and unwilling to take risks.

A rider I knew had once been very confident: when he had something new to try, he made a picture of himself succeeding, then felt good about it, and tried it out. Often, his confidence carried him through, but when he wasn't very successful he reminded himself that he didn't have to be perfect the first time. In other words, when he was less successful, his pattern was to add a cheerfully encouraging piece of internal dialogue to his evaluation of what had happened. Then he moved to another area, and had to change his teacher. This one was much less encouraging, more critical, than his old one, saying things like 'Watch out that you don't…', 'Mind that he doesn't…', 'You'll probably find this difficult the first time…' and so on. It didn't take very long for this rider to lose his confidence. When we looked at the internal sequence of the new kind of thinking he had got into, we found that the old pattern of:

picture (V) ► good feeling (K) ► try it out
had been changed. Now it was:
picture (V) ► internal dialogue (ID) about the difficulty he would be facing ► anxious feeling (K) ► less confident behaviour.

His teacher's habitual negativity had been heard so often that he had incorporated it into his own thought pattern, developing a self-limiting loop which interfered with his performance. We experimented with different ways of changing this. Initially, he found it worked if he continued the internal dialogue a little longer, reminding himself that if we are to learn we have to experiment, and that it is okay not to be perfect. This was enough to change how he felt about trying. After a while, he found he had reverted to his old, more self-confident pattern. He didn't need this teacher's perfectionism limiting him inside his head. He also changed his teacher for one whose approach suited him more!

Modelling

NLP was built on modelling: by asking excellent practitioners **how** they did things the founders of NLP gathered information about all kinds of internal and external processes. They began to assemble the equivalent of recipes for each of the specific people they studied – and then to draw from these a set of general recipes which underlie the workings of all of them. It's rather like collecting the recipes for different kinds of sauces, and then realising that *all* sauces have some things in common. Thus it became possible to explain both the general patterns and how they were individually varied.

The process of modelling individuals has a great deal to offer us as riders. In the profile of Charles de Kunffy later in the book I have tried to answer some 'how' questions: how does he get into an appropriate state for teaching; how does he ensure that he explains things in a way which reaches all the riders he teaches; how does he keep in mind what he wants each rider and horse to achieve when he his judging or teaching? In the interviews I have had with him, and in observing him give many lessons over the years, I have continually been asking the question 'How?'

The more detailed the answers we get, when we ask this question, the more useful the information. We can model the excellence of others, and we can also model ourselves. By asking the kinds of questions outlined in this book, we can find out a great deal about how we go about things: how we do what works, and how we do what doesn't. Both have a structure; and the structure will have some things in common with other people's, and in some ways be unique to us. Success has a structure; so does panic; so do fear, and anxiety, and confidence. But your fear, and your confidence, will not be exactly the same as mine, or as your friend with the horse in the next box. And it's yours which count, for you.

When we observe someone who is truly excellent, it can feel impossible to model so much. Like all tasks, modelling is best done bit by bit. You can model anything that someone does well. Perhaps a friend is really good at plaiting – how does she do that? Someone else may be very calm at shows – how does he do that? Your horse will pee on command – how did you get him to do that? Your trainer always finds something to praise and to build on – how does she do that? You will find that most people are only too pleased to tell you how they go about things: often, they haven't thought about it in that much detail themselves, and they find it a fascinating learning experience too. Ask them at a time when they are free to reflect, and when you can make detailed notes. It's the exact detail you are after, preferably in their own words. And if you listen carefully to the words, they will often tell you exactly what processes are going on inside. For example: '*Well, first I look at the mane, and divide it into plaits* **in my mind's eye** *(V), and then I take a chunk of hair that* **feels about right** *(K) and put a rubber band around it…*'

When you model someone, you are really asking them to teach you how they do what they do. Here are some suggestions for the kinds of things you can say:

External behaviour

Describe to me…

Show me…

What do you do…?

If I were watching you, how would I know you were doing it?

How do you start doing this?

How do you stop doing it?

How would I do it?

Internal State

How do you feel as you do X?

What do you feel as you do X?

What do you need to feel in order to do X?

If they are demonstrating it

What are you feeling inside?

What emotions, if any, are you aware of as you do this?

Are you aware of any smells, any tastes?

Internal processing

What do you see externally as you do X?

What do you hear externally as you do X?

What are you thinking as you do X?

Do you have any internal pictures?

Do you have any internal dialogue?

What do you say to yourself as you do X?

Context

Where, when, with whom, how long… do you do X?

Where, when, with whom, how long… do you not do X?

Cause and effect

How do you know when to do X?

What lets you know it is appropriate to do X at this time?

What makes you do X?

What will cause you to do X?

What would stop you from doing X?

The meaning of X to the doer

What is important about doing this?

What does doing this satisfy for you/in you?

As you are doing this what does it fulfil/satisfy in yourself?

Why are you doing this?

Why do you do this?

[Questions adapted from ITS NLP Master Practitioner Training]

The test of modelling is that you have got enough information, and the right kind of information, to teach the skill to someone else. If you have, you have modelled successfully. If not, the experience of trying will show you what further information you need: it will be a process of feedback.

In these first two chapters I have introduced some NLP concepts and skills which can help us as riders, explaining the nature and uses of some of the key items in the tool-kit. Now it is time to look at some of the problems which we face in our riding, and how these tools can help us more specifically.

Solving Problems in Rider-Horse Communication

The horse could and did give man a total education. He had to be tamed and befriended, and could not be fooled by honeyed words. Thus, only those who had the humility to blame failures on themselves and never on their mount could benefit from the education a horse could offer.

CHARLES DE KUNFFY *The Ethics and Passions of Dressage*

The horse knows no right from wrong and learns everything indiscriminately. Therefore, in schooling there is no neutrality.

CHARLES DE KUNFFY *The Ethics and Passions of Dressage*

CHAPTER 3

What's it Like to be Your Horse?

The horse has the neurological aptitude to react to very slight stimuli. He has the mental aptitude to perceive for a sustained period of time very mild stimuli, and to differentiate between them. He has an excellent memory.
CHARLES DE KUNFFY *The Ethics and Passions of Dressage*

Imagine what the relationship is like from the other person's point of view. This is going to second position. How do they experience your behaviour?
O'CONNOR AND MCDERMOTT *Principles of NLP*

We understand the world on the basis of what our senses tell us and what we decide this 'means'. So does everyone else – and we know how many misunderstandings that can lead to! In training and riding horses, we have the additional problem that they see and understand the world differently from us, and we will never be able to share their experience exactly.

The word 'misunderstanding' is interesting, since it implies that there is a fixed something to be understood and that one or both parties to the exchange has or have in some way got it wrong. It is more helpful, I believe, to think instead of understandings which are 'mismatched': there are good reasons why each party understands what he or she does – but they do not correspond.

However, NLP offers us some important ways to improve our understanding on the basis of the evidence we do have. This chapter outlines some tools which help specifically with understanding what our actions mean to our horses – so that we can be sure of giving them the messages we intend. This means that we can clear up mismatched understandings, arguments, frustrations and distress on both sides.

Presuppositions

Three NLP presuppositions are particularly relevant here:

- The meaning of a communication is the message received.

- Behaviour is the best quality information.

- There is no failure, only feedback.

The meaning of a communication is the message received

As many an argument the world over has demonstrated, what matters to a person is what *they* thought you said, or did, not what *you* thought. So far as they are concerned, what they understood is what you actually meant. When I was a teenager, living in London, my father and I arranged to meet each other at a certain Underground station. I went down to the platform we needed: my father waited in the booking hall. After some time he came down and found me. Then we had a row about what 'meeting at the station' meant!

Like much of NLP, this presupposition is value-free: it describes what is the case, not what *ought to be* or should be or might be. If we take it on board, it can relieve us of much worry and self-blame: it directs us away from guilt, remorse, anger, digging in the past which we can no longer influence, towards the possibility of real choices about action in the present. The question it presents to us is *what do we need to do now to ensure that the 'receiver' gets the message we do intend?*

Behaviour is the best quality information

'Actions speak louder than words' – a saying so familiar that we can easily forget its real practical guidance. If we really notice the actions of other people we gain access to another layer of meaning beside what is actually said. Examples are what we now call 'Freudian slips' of the tongue, accidental 'forgetting', 'mistakes' and so on: the unintentional give-aways which Freud was the first to write about but which people have always done – and caught each other out in doing! Behaviour tells us important things about the other person (horse) who is doing the behaving, and from earliest childhood we are experts in making interpretations of it. This does not mean, of course, that our interpretations are always right, because our own habits of sifting and interpreting evidence can filter or distort it.

'Behaviour is the best quality information'. Whilst active, Lolly is responding to my rigidity by hollowing and coming above the bit. The well-developed muscle under his neck shows that, at this time, he was often in this posture.

It can be really helpful to remember that a horse's behaviour is always telling us something about what is going on for him. His behaviour – everyday and unusual, repeated or uncommon, tells us about his world. And so it tells us a lot about how he understands us and our impact on his world. The more we ignore this evidence, or overlook it because of our own assumptions, the more we limit ourselves and our learning. If we assume that a horse is 'resistant' or 'lazy', for example, we will tend to look no further for explanations of his unwillingness to go forward, or to accept the bit, or whatever is the behaviour bothering us. Investigating both habitual and infrequent behaviour for possible meanings can be very fruitful, and can help us target our actions more effectively towards what we *would* like the horse to understand and to do.

There is no failure, only feedback

This is another really useful presupposition, because it reframes the meaning of things turning out differently from how we hoped or intended. 'Failure' almost always leads to bad, or sad, feelings – and these in turn affect not only what we do next but how we do it. If our horse 'won't go on the bit', and we feel that we have somehow failed in our training, or our management of our hands, we may feel angry, disappointed, or inadequate. This in turn will affect how we behave, and because our feelings will be communicated to the horse a sequence and perhaps even a loop may result.

A horse I knew would not stand to be mounted: as soon as the rider picked up the reins and went to mount, he backed away or swung his quarters sideways. As he was otherwise a cooperative horse, it seemed likely that he had had some bad experience being mounted in the past. His new owner, who was extremely competent, but sometimes lacked self-confidence, became anxious after the horse 'flipped' one day while she was mounting, and bucked repetitively until he got her off. Her anxiety and sense of failure, not unnaturally, was picked up by the horse, who then became even more restless. Another rider, visiting the yard, was asked to exercise him: she was 'not bothered' by his behaviour, remained calm and acted rather bored each time he moved, and after three or four fidgets he allowed her to get on.

The point is certainly not that the one rider was in any way 'better' than the other – rather that two riders of more or less equal competence had quite different experiences in the 'same' situation. The one who had been thrown off became understandably anxious that this would happen again, felt a failure because she could not find an effective way of preventing it, and was in danger of reinforcing the horse's own fear. She felt the situation was threatening, and effectively 'told' the horse that he was right to fear it. The other rider (who admittedly hadn't been thrown off) was able to treat the horse's behaviour as a minor, rather tedious, difficulty, so in effect telling him that the situation was not as dangerous as he feared.

If we take this example further, we might say: well, didn't that make the owner even more upset – and yes, it did. But taking the episode as feedback, she was able to remember other things which made the horse anxious and to ask herself honestly what kind of horse she really wanted. She decided she needed a horse who would match not just her dressage ambitions but also her temperament – one she could 'play with' as well as compete. So she began to consider selling this one – not because she had 'failed', but because there was a significant mismatch between them.

I read in an issue of *Dressage News* about a high-level dressage horse who was brilliant in competition but horrid in the stable – biting and kicking out and difficult to tack up. From the tone of his owner's comments, she regarded this, quite affectionately, as part of the 'person' he was. I wouldn't want that kind of horse myself: it wouldn't suit my nature or what I want to do with my horses. Personally, I would sacrifice brilliance in the arena for a horse I can trust everywhere I am with him: in the school, in the stable, hacking as well as in the arena. Sometimes it just isn't worth taking on all that might be involved: if we clear the idea of failure from our minds we can decide what we really want.

Meanings: the Value of Shifting Position

It seems that all intelligent creatures make some kind of meaning out of their experience: they respond to patterns by expecting them to be repeated; they like certain things and fear others. Those who are capable of being trained have shown that they can link actions with situations or commands. Some kinds of meanings are pre-programmed: horses have evolved as herd-members and prey-animals, used to company and hierarchies, and with an acute awareness of their surroundings and an instinctive readiness to take flight. But they don't filter information in the same way as we do, as the quote from de Kunffy at the beginning of this section points out: *they learn everything*. When they do filter, it is in relation to *their* built-in purposes, not ours!

As riders, we need to be very aware of this. Our horses learn not only what we intend them to learn but much else besides – including things we would rather they did not learn. And sometimes even what we intend to teach them doesn't turn out to be such a bright idea, either.

When we had our first horse, someone thought of teaching him to 'shake hands' in exchange for an apple after being ridden. He was a quick learner, raising his off fore obediently when told to 'shake'. But his learning didn't stop there: so far as he was concerned, raising his 'paw' *brought* an apple – how about raising it when he *wanted* an apple? This was indeed a bright idea – but less good from the point of the humans around him. Irritating, and even potentially dangerous at times. As new owners, we simply hadn't thought it through.

As owners and trainers, we have two kinds of learning (meaning-making) available to us: the meanings which are naturally bred into the horse, which we may need to work around or make use of, and those which they learn intentionally or unintentionally from our behaviour. Every action and reaction offers an opportunity: they can't *not* learn because we can't *not* communicate.

This gives us pause for thought. We may, for example, ignore something because we are in a hurry, or something else is more important to us. We might dodge past the horse standing in his doorway one day if in a hurry to skip out, rather than insisting he backs away to give us room: but what if on another occasion it is important – or even a matter of safety – that he back up, and he has learnt that we do not always 'mean' it? We have avoided immediate conflict – at the expense of teaching him long-term that he can ignore us and the rules we set because we aren't always consistent.

If behaviour is the best source of information, its friend is the ability to do what NLP calls '**shifting position**' – a process which our parents began to drum into us when, as little children, they exasperatedly asked us: 'How would you feel if that was done to you?' The position we all start from, is known in NLP as **First Position:** I; me; how I think, feel, see the world. Learning to imagine how the world is for others is to take **Second Position:** asking ourselves how they think, feel, experience, whether it is the same situation we are in, or whether we are considering something in the past or something as yet in the future. There is also a very useful **Third Position**, which is one of a detached observer watching the situation, standing back from the feelings, seeing ourselves as others might see us, perhaps gaining access to the opinions and knowledge of a 'wiser self'.

This chapter is really all about the need to take second position with our horses: it is one of the most important ways of checking out two vital things: first, what they are likely to be experiencing and learning, and, second, specifically how they may be experiencing and understanding us and what we do. So it has two kinds of payoff: in terms of our caring, it ensures that we monitor what goes on around them for its impact on them; and in terms of effectiveness as trainers and riders, it allows us a way of checking up on ourselves.

So, take a few moments next time you are in the yard to pretend that you are your horse. What is going on around him? What effects might it be having? What sights, sounds, smells, movements might he be aware of? What might he be learning from them? Horses are creatures of habit, and he will be used to the normal patterns of the yard. Like you, he will unconsciously calibrate any differences and react to what they mean to him: for example, he will know there

Rider thinks:
(1st Position) *'He's never done this before. What a fool I feel.'*

(2nd Position) *'If I were him, I'd find all those flowers and that hut a bit much, too.'*

(3rd Position) *'Still, at least it's given the judge a good laugh.'*

is a show coming up, not just because someone has bathed and plaited him but because of changes in tempo around the yard. People may be moving faster; their voice tone may differ from that of an 'ordinary day'. Perhaps he is aware of a loss of your attention – as you groom him you may not be talking to him as much as you usually do because you are distracted by trying to remember if you have got everything ready, or worrying about whether you will be ready on time; perhaps you are impatient when he moves because you are trying to plait, or bandage his tail, so that a fidget you would normally put up with suddenly irritates you. From things like these he will certainly know that something different is afoot! He may become tetchier or wound up himself. Chapter Nine, on Competition, looks more fully at these and other problems associated with competing.

While we may think of 'around the yard' as being different – perhaps even very different – from being 'in the school', your horse may well not make such a distinction. So far as he is concerned, he has been standing about all day, thinking equine thoughts or half-asleep, and suddenly you arrive, throw his clothes on and expect him to get out in the school and work. Do you? Or are you aware that a transition needs to be made – that he needs to stretch, warm up his muscles, focus his attention? Are there ever times when you are so keen to get a movement right that you repeat it endlessly – just one more half-pass? What meaning is he making from this? Perhaps that nothing is ever good enough for you; perhaps, if you ask him to go on working in a particular gait or outline even when his muscles are tired and he is showing this by irritability, 'gobbiness' or stiffness, that you don't care how he feels. What would you be experiencing if you were in his shoes?

We all forget sometimes to step into second position and check what might be going on there. Usually this is because we are stuck in our first person concerns and anxieties. It's not always even for reasons of selfishness, either. I was watching a friend riding her young horse one day, and asked how he was going. She said that he was rather stiff and resistant, even though she had had a brilliant session on him the day before. Then, he had worked in collection and balance with a great deal of suppleness and energy. She had been so pleased and had looked forward to today... Something reminded me of the times when I used to go to a health club to exercise: the staff advised us that we should only work out every other day, to give the hard-worked muscles time to rest, reconstitute and rebuild. The space between sessions, they said, was a vital part of building strength. Standing by the school, I wondered if this young horse might need the same kind of rebuilding time. I suggested that maybe he was tired from the previous schooling session: what about working him long and low for a few minutes to stretch, then calling it a day. My friend thought this might be a good idea. With evident relief her horse stretched forward and down into the longer frame, and within a minute or two was swinging along in good rhythm, his back working freely with returned energy. His stiffness and resistance had been expressing his tiredness and his need for a longer frame. How else could he have told her?

'His stiffness and resistance had been expressing his tiredness and his need for a longer frame. How else could he have told her?'

Let's take some other examples. First, patting. As a judge, I see a lot of it, when the final halt and salute have been done and the rider wants to thank the horse. What the rider usually does is to thump or slap the horse loudly on the neck, perhaps several times. The rider is pleased; the rider's voice tells the horse of this pleasure – in words and in its tone. But what does the slap mean to him? What does it mean at other times, when someone is cross with him for not moving out of the way, for snatching at his dinner, for nipping? Watching both Charles de Kunffy and Arthur Kottas training horses over the years, I have often been struck by how quiet and minimal their touching is, even when they are saying thank-you to a horse for good behaviour or hard work. A short, smooth sliding caress on the neck says 'thank you' in a very different way, one which could not possibly be confused with a blow or smack. When I talked about this with Charles, his view was that 'patting' was invasive and quite unnecessary: why should a horse have to learn to reinterpret being struck as an act of affection? Why not just use a movement that clearly, and immediately, means just what it says?

While patting is very specific, we can usefully consider a much more complex set of messages we give the horse: the messages of aiding. The most obvious

A short, smooth, gliding caress on the neck.

meaning – so far as we are concerned, is that we are telling the horse what we want. But let's look at this from the horse's point of view. De Kunffy sometimes tells a rider: '*Give him a tap with the whip– you know he loves it!*' I have often been puzzled by this, but it terms of NLP it makes a great deal of sense. If the tap is just that, a tap, what does it say? It says ' hey, wake up'; but over and beyond that it tells the horse that *you are paying attention to him*.

All of us have probably had the experience of talking to someone and suddenly realising we have 'lost them' – that their attention has wandered. Body-language gives us many slight signals; if we are facing them we may see their faces go blank or their eyes defocus – universally recognised signals that the person has 'gone off somewhere in their head'. I believe this is the kind of experience our horses have when we just allow them to dawdle along. They have lost us. The lack of reaction, the lack of aiding, tells them that.

Aiding is a word whose meaning has become so familiar that it has almost disappeared. If we bring it into our attention again, we see that the messages we give our horse are intended to help him know what he is doing and guide him as to what he should do. They are there for his support. A tap with the whip, an adjustment of the weight, a flexion in our shoulders, a feel on the wrist, are small, subtle messages that reassure him 'I am here, I notice, I care' as well as 'do this, do that'.

Like many idealistic (soft?) riders, I have always wanted my hands to be gentle, the feel on the rein minimal. It has taken me a long time - and an understanding of NLP – to heed what my trainers have said: that horses need 'support' through the contact and that it needs to be consistent. If my contact comes and goes, he can't find me. If I give away the outside rein, he has nothing to work into. Worse, I may alternate between offering him some contact, none or too much if he stretches forward or I accidentally grab the rein. If I don't set the length of the frame, he has no endpoint to create what Burger calls the *bow before the saddle;* if my leg and seat are weak or inconsistent, there is no base from which he can create the *bow behind the saddle.* This is a metaphor which draws our attention to the connection between the muscle groups which raise the neck from the wither, suspending the head rather than propping it up, and those which correspondingly raise the back under the rider, providing an elastic cushion upon which to suspend the rider and absorb the impacts of the rider's weight.

The need to create this double bow does not give me a licence for strong contact, relentless legs or a driving and flattening seat: far from it. But it has made me aware that I need to consider what my horse is actually experiencing as a result of my beliefs. And that sometimes he may be experiencing something I would not intend. Since I am 'the smart partner on the back of the strong partner', as de Kunffy expresses it, I have the responsibility for monitoring what is going on: only I have the ability to take second position and check out from my imagination, and from careful consideration of my horse's behaviour, what he is taking in. It is my responsibility to help him to understand.

Some of these meanings affect the horse's mind and feelings – reassurance, attentiveness; others are intended solely or mainly for his body, and I shall return to those later in this chapter.

Attentiveness, mutual attentiveness, is the basis of all good relationships. It conveys care and respect; it allows us to make subtle adjustments to our actions and responses, to create what Burger called 'a conversation at a higher level'. All the great practitioners of dressage have used this metaphor of conversation in their writings. How can we have a good conversation unless we are both paying attention to each other?

This brings a new layer of meaning to our training around the yard. If we expect horses to be attentive to us, and respectful of us, around the yard, and if we respect them in the same way, we are laying a foundation for a seamless communication in the whole of our relationship together. If we disrupt them by shouting to friends across the yard, we damage that respectfulness, and we model disruptiveness to them. If we let them barge when we take them in or out of their boxes, or when we muck out, we are making it harder for them to learn that respect for each other's space is a condition of the relationship. Being aware of what our actions may mean to the horse is not a licence for indulging him, but a vital guideline. As one of my trainers used to say, 'You're paying his keep: he has to work for it'. But equally, without him I could not be a rider, so I have to work for it too.

Distortions of Meaning

In any of our communications with others, human or equine, we are dealing with many items of information – more, in fact, than the human brain is capable of processing at any one time. We take in so much through all of our senses that the conscious mind is overloaded, and relies on simplification in order to cope. While the simplification is essential for living life, it can also be the source of problems, and NLP shows us some useful ways to watch out for these pitfalls and to guard against them.

There are three main ways in which we simplify the evidence which comes to us through our senses. They are

- Deletion

- Distortion

- Generalisation.

Each of these can cause problems for us as riders.

Deletion

Deletion means that, in becoming aware of a situation, we overlook or leave out some of the available information. We may do this deliberately, but more often we have learnt to automatically rule out certain kinds of information as irrelevant. In our experience, there will be good reasons for this – but ignoring information means that we may lose meanings it could give us.

For example, a rider was talking in the tackroom about how much better her horse was going since she had bought him a new bit, recommended by a well-known trainer who had given her a lesson. A friend, listening to the conversation, asked the teacher if her horse would also benefit from this miraculous bit. The teacher said she thought he did not need one, as he was already quite prepared to work towards the bit. Not entirely convinced, and feeling that she needed all the help she could get in establishing a more harmonious relationship through the rein, the second owner later borrowed the bit and tried it out: in fact her horse did go much better in it, and so she bought one.

The teacher was not wrong in her assessment of the horse, but she did overlook (delete) some of the available information in reaching her judgement. The bit was a more tasty one – and she did not know whether or not this would appeal to the second horse. In addition, while the horse went kindly to the bit when she was riding him he was not always so accepting when the owner rode.

Distortion

Usually, we distort meaning because we filter it through what we believe (we may do this with deletion, too). Any belief is a theory about experience, rather than a fact; but we tend to behave as though our beliefs are facts – and that is the problem. If we believe that mares are 'mareish', we will tend to notice behaviour in them which confirms this belief. We may also fail to correct it because we believe that it is not correctable. (The same goes for the kind of 'boys will be boys' beliefs people have about humans, too.) With a well-entrenched belief, we will also tend to be less aware of information which contradicts it. Most of the time, we are fond of our horses, and get used to their way of going – but this may distort our perception of them.

> For example, a horse being ridden as a guinea-pig at a dressage clinic was rushing along with short, flat steps. As the trainer worked with the rider, asking her to slow the horse and to ask her to rebalance, the rider several times commented, a little defensively, that her horse was nice-natured, helpful, willing, cooperative. The trainer pointed out that however nice the horse was she shouldn't be let off the hook or not asked to work more correctly!

Generalisation

Generalisation is an essential part of learning. When we generalise from one or two experiences of something – see a pattern and learn to expect or anticipate it – we save a great deal of time and effort. *Look right, look left, look right again* gives us a way of managing traffic – until we go abroad. In riding, generalisation helps us in similar ways, and in similar ways it can get in the way of new, or contradictory, evidence. It can mean that in riding a new horse, for example, we may expect him to respond as our old one did; it can also mean that we make assumptions about riding or training on the basis of previous experience or fixed beliefs which may not be borne out this time around. Generalisation always involves a belief, because essentially what we have done is to form a general understanding on the basis of only a few experiences. If we assume, for example, that all horses are essentially lazy, our treatment of each new one we meet will be strongly influenced by trying to bypass or deal with the resistances we expect.

> Another example might be that when a horse is showing temper, or not going forward, many riders will assume that it is their own fault (trainers may agree, unless they belong to the 'horses are lazy' brigade). Yet, as the Expert Answers columns in the horse magazines often point out, temper and resistance often relate to pain in teeth, jaw or back: these are the first things to check. If we generalise that such problems are likely to be the rider's fault, we may miss other crucial factors – and unwittingly prolong both our horse's discomfort and his behavioural problems.

In identifying these mental coping mechanisms NLP is not telling us that they are wrong – only that we need to be aware of how they can get between us and our ability to observe and evaluate what is going on. By and large, such processes serve us usefully; but next time you have a problem in communication it may be worth checking if one of these has been involved.

Working with In-built Meanings

I talked earlier in the chapter about the possible negative meanings to the horse of a 'minimalist' contact, and of how aiding can help or hinder him to use his physiology correctly. While this book is not about dressage techniques, it is important to point out that the systematic classical training which developed over many centuries was based on an understanding of the in-built physiological meanings of the horse's structure and function. The greatest riding masters over the years evolved a programme of what the rider had to do in order to assist the horse to build the musculature and the flexibility that would help him carry his rider effectively and without strain. That is the meaning of 'classical' riding: it is *a system which already works*. NLP sets out to describe 'what works'; and classical equitation exemplifies the modelling of excellence from generation to generation.

Let's look briefly here at some of the key features of the rider's physical communication to the horse.

I have already mentioned the concept of the bow before the saddle and the bow behind it. How does the rider activate the bow? By a deep seat which massages the muscle groups of the back; by stabilising the hands through elbows kept close to the rider's sides rather than moving loosely and erratically without that attachment; by activating the horse's hind legs with legs and seat so as to bring them under the horse, raising his forehand and allowing him to lift himself instead of just propelling himself along. The core features of the classical seat can be shown to derive from what they actually achieve. They are correct – but correct because they communicate effectively, helping the horse to move and carry himself in a way which benefits him, averts unnecessary wear and strain, and so prolongs his life as well as making it more comfortable.

Every feature of correct rider positioning contributes to this. The lowered heel and raised toe ensure that the calf muscle is raised against the horse, thus making it effective. The tilt of the pelvis so that its base is slightly more forward allows the rider's back to remain soft and to swing with the movement, encouraging elevation and impulsion rather than suppressing them. The upright carriage of the head ('Look up! look up!' the trainer repeats – often fruitlessly)

The core features of the classical seat. Debby and Merlin.

means that the rider's weight is distributed down the spine and deflected outward either side of the horse's back, whereas tipping it forward would bring the rider's shoulders and weight forward, so loading the horse's shoulders. The stability of the rider's elbows against the body helps produce a light, following yet constantly supportive contact because the rider doesn't have to carry the weight of the forearms from the shoulder muscles. De Kunffy is fond of saying that 'the rider's upper arm and elbows belong to her sides: her hands belong to her horse'. Close examination of the classical position, and classical aiding, demonstrates how the trained rider can speak to the horse in ways which give him the most opportunity of understanding and obeying, because these ways are based on how he himself functions. As I shall explain further in the next chapter, the rider is **matching and pacing** the horse – which establishes the best position from which to influence or **lead** him. To borrow the title of another book on NLP, this is truly to be ***Influencing with Integrity***: the rider does indeed wish to influence the horse, but working from within the classical perspective influences him in a way which respects both his personal and his physiological integrity.

This respectful attitude, communicated as effectively as we can through our dealings with the horse in the yard and in the school, is the basis of earning the attentiveness and the trust from him which are essential for completing the communication between us. This is the key to what the dressage sheets call 'submission': a true willingness to set aside many natural instincts (such as flight) and to be attentive and responsive to the rider. It is a submission which can only be freely given, not demanded but earned.

Ray, an elderly friend of ours, started his schoolteaching career in a remote area of New Zealand. The transport provided for him was a horse, who took him to school each day and spent the school hours in the adjoining field. If Ray wanted to go to the cinema or the pub in the nearest township, he had to ride there and back, which involved crossing the many convoluted streams of one of New Zealand's 'braided' rivers. On one such occasion, a storm with heavy rain began during the evening, and by the time Ray set out for home it was pitch black and the river was rising in flood. The familiar landmarks were invisible or covered by rising water. On reaching the first of the river banks, Ray gave his horse a loose rein and hoped for the best: he had no option but to trust Major – and Major picked his way safely through the waters and got him home. His care in getting Ray home was also shown from time to time in less dramatic circumstances – when an evening at the pub, for example, had rendered Ray's aids rather less than precise!

In a recent conversation I had with Charles de Kunffy, he told me how as a young man he had been competing in a strenuous long-distance ride. He and his horse were both overcome with exhaustion. Charles described how – foolishly as he now thinks – he lay down 'for a moment' beside his sitting horse, leaning against the shoulder in the hollow behind the curled front leg. He was awakened some time later by a repeated nuzzling. Only once he had struggled awake, and got to his feet, did the horse get up: the horse had urgently needed to stale, but had woken Charles before getting up himself. Because of their mutual trust, the horse had learnt to put the safety of his rider before his own needs. Perhaps we might even say that in this case he was showing an ability to take second position?

Many riders will have similar stories, illustrating two way trust and affection which go far beyond mere obedience or 'submission'. I believe that if we make a habit, as owners and as riders, of imagining ourselves into the shoes of our horses we will gain invaluable insight into the world that they experience – which includes our impact on them. 'Second-positioning' in this way gives us the means of checking out what they think we mean – and how far this might correspond, or deviate, from what we intend. It is a non-judgemental way of testing, and improving, our effectiveness in building this sometimes elusive, yet essentially remarkable and inspiring partnership with our horses.

CHAPTER 4

The Four Basics:
Rapport, Outcomes, Sensory Acuity, Experimentation (ROSE)

A rider should always be fully aware of the horse's well-being and his horse's communications. He must also react to them with knowledge and insight. Knowledge comes by practicing riding, coaching, reading, watching and discussing. More important, however, is the insight and wisdom gained by empathy towards the horse. Empathy, putting it simply, is the ability to put oneself into the position of another, to focus on the needs and interests of another rather than on one's own. The most sophisticated behaviour, the most civilised and mature inner life of any person, is based on his ability to be 'outward' rather than 'inward'. The rider ought to train himself to think the way his horse does.

CHARLES DE KUNFFY *Training Strategies for Dressage Riders*

Effective communication begins with the recognition that each of us is unique and different…Good communication skills bridge those differences. Bridging skills are influencing skills: they increase understanding and improve the quality of the goals of each individual in the communication process.

GENIE Z. LABORDE *Influencing with Integrity*

In this chapter I shall explore what have been called the 'four pillars' of NLP, because they are at the heart of good communication.

R = RAPPORT

O = OUTCOMES

S = SENSORY ACUITY

E = EXPERIMENTATION

First, a brief exploration of what each involves, then a fuller exploration of how this relates to us as riders.

Rapport is a two-way bonding between individuals. Often, it happens quite spontaneously, as between friends. But NLP shows us how it can also created deliberately – and still be just as genuine.

Outcomes We often know what we want, but unless an item on our wish-list meets certain conditions it may be doomed to failure. The NLP search for 'what works' has identified key factors which can help us load our goals for success.

Sensory acuity If we want to get better at anything, we need to notice more, and be able to act on finer detail. This sharp awareness of information we receive through our different senses is what is meant by 'sensory acuity'. NLP has some really useful tools to help us notice more, and faster, and to act quickly and effectively on the information we are receiving.

Experimentation Flexibility is the fourth key to good communication, and thus to sorting out problems and blocks.

We might think of these as being rather like the pillars in the centre of the Spanish Riding School, between which the most highly schooled horses perform the most skilled movements with such ease, fluency and balance that they appear effortless even if remarkable. Good communication is like that – between people or between rider and horse. Remembering its four key elements through the convenient acronym of the ROSE will help us develop our ability to communicate until it, too, attains that apparent effortlessness.

Rapport

What is rapport, and how can we achieve it in riding? Rapport begins with observation. As I showed in the last chapter, by watching the 'other' (in our case, the horse) carefully we can begin to know about his 'model of the world' – what he likes, what he is afraid of, his individual character and responses. Against that background of his usual patterns we can note the variations and differences. Is he tired today (how do we know?). Is he unwell, or apprehensive, excited or bored? This is how we observe the people in our lives, too, and how we 'know' that they are angry, or upset, or flustered, even without being told. The ability respectfully to take account of both 'normal' patterns and variations from them forms the basis of rapport.

Horses, being prey-animals, are great observers too – their peripheral vision ensures that they are quick to spot the smallest movement. They have good hearing. They are herd animals, and used to paying attention to the others in their herd (which includes us!). They don't miss much that we do around them. This means that we have many, many opportunities for communication with them, in the field and the stable, not just when saddled up. In fact, we cannot help communicating *something* every time we are in their presence. The skills which NLP offers us help us to ensure that more of our communication is what we actually *intend*.

I was once out hacking on a bridleway and came across a tree which had fallen right across the path. There were some broken branches sticking out, but there was also room to jump between them, and the total height of the obstacle was only about 18 inches. Lolly, our middle-aged schoolmaster, was often dubious about jumps when first presented to them, but then enjoyed discovering his adventurous side. He stopped dead when he saw this fallen tree, and I persuaded him to walk up to look at it, intending then to walk away again and give him a short run-up. However, once he had looked at it he voluntarily jumped it from a standstill and then cantered off gaily, clearly telling me that he felt no end of a fellow.

As with people, we build rapport with horses if we show them that we understand what it is like to be them. This includes both obvious things like not making sudden movements or loud noises around them, and also more subtle ones like taking account of their individual natures. A timid horse, like a timid person, is unlikely to learn greater boldness through being hurried, urged or forced to do things. Charles de Kunffy makes the point that effective training happens when the rider/trainer so organises things that the horse finds it easy or inevitable to do the desired behaviour and thinks it was his idea in the first place. In this case, I respected my horse's natural caution, and he then surprised me by volunteering what I really wanted.

Our younger horse, Vals, always showed some tension about upward transitions to canter. As a youngster, he would get anxious and become hollow. Later, when he learnt to relax more and remain 'through' for single transitions, he was still worried about doing simple changes.

Our trainer, Debby, found when she was training and competing him that it was counterproductive to be firm with him when he hesitated or even began to back off her aids at these moments. It only made him more anxious. What did work was for her to remain calm and wait the few moments it took him to sort himself out and go forward again in his own time. This change in her approach made a difference in the space of one week from test marks of 2 for the simple changes in Medium tests to marks of 5 at the next competition – an improvement which continued.

We don't know why Vals became anxious about canter transitions in the first place, although some back and neck problems he had once had may have caused his fear originally. Even though the physical problems were sorted out, his fear remained – and he needed time to dismantle it. But looking at the problem from an NLP viewpoint, we can see that the loss of rapport with his rider when she tried to urge him on just made the problem worse. Once she allowed him to sort the timing out himself, encouraging him passively rather than actively, he was able to do the rest. Keeping rapport with him gave him the confidence to go on – literally!

Since we can't explain our ideas and intentions in words to our horses, we have to explain in 'language' they do understand, using body-mind events such as posture, gesture, breathing, energy, voice-tone and rhythm. The trainer Monty Roberts began his observations of horses as a young boy, watching wild horses in the desert when he was stalking them in order to catch them. Because of his hatred of the breaking methods used by his father and other trainers, he became interested in how the young horses were trained by the older ones to become acceptable herd members. Watching in the still of the night, alone in the wilderness, he noticed how the dominant mare would either ignore boisterous behaviour by the young horses or deliberately drive them to the edges of the herd. After a while their need to belong would impel them into calm and submissive behaviour, signalled by a lowering of the head and a chewing movement of the lips and jaw. Only then would the dominant mare admit the youngster to the herd. Roberts found that by copying the mare's behaviour he, too, could persuade wild horses to seek a relationship with him, and that the 'joining' pattern was the same.

By first joining them in their map of the world, he created a situation in which they volunteered to join him in his. In his written work, his demonstrations and his videos he shows how this process works time and again. His work is unusual not just because of what he does, but because of his meticulous analysis of *how* it works. He demonstrates that an effective process can be observed, analysed, described and taught.

A rider had a yearling, who injured her foot and had to be taken away from her friends in the field and stabled for several weeks while the foot was treated and had time to heal. The filly had been handled in the field, but not much. The owner now handled the yearling daily, grooming her and accustoming her to a headcollar and to being tied up in the box and the yard. One day, she decided to experiment. The yearling accepted a surcingle, four leg bandages and a tail bandage, and walked calmly round the yard with all this new gear on.

The owner began by matching the yearling's need for belonging and for touch. In the field with two other youngsters and with older mares, she had been used to physical contact. The youngsters regularly groom each other, and even a stiff brush is gentler than teeth! Being away from her friends, she missed contact, and transferred her dependence on friendship to her owner and other people around the yard. Handled every day, the filly was quite happy to accept the bandages and surcingle. The owner 'piggybacked' the communication the filly was used to, and simply took it further.

The little filly understood from her owner's behaviour that bandages and surcingle were just other ways of telling her that she belonged. We can predict that the rest of her training process will be presented and received in the same way. One way of summarising this is to say that *we can tell when we are in rapport with a horse when he appears to be in rapport with us.*

- List some examples from your own experience (however small or insignificant they may appear to be) of times when your horse appeared to be in rapport with you. What details of his behaviour indicated rapport? Now examine your own behaviour to find out how, in fact, you may have first shown him that you were in rapport with him.

Let's imagine that a young horse in the early stages of schooling is trotting around the school. Through exuberance, or being slightly startled, he breaks into canter. The rider says 'no' and brings him back to trot.

*The rider **intends** to tell the horse 'Only canter when I ask you'. The horse may think she means 'don't canter', which can cause hesitation later in making upward transitions.*

The young horse canters, unasked. The rider accepts the canter and rides a movement (for example, a circuit or large circle) before asking for a trot again.

This rider is telling the horse: 'Canter is good, we can work with this'. Then she asks for trot, and rewards the horse when he accepts that aid. The horse gets a clear sign of acceptance for cantering in itself, and then a reward for accepting the downward aid. By not correcting the canter, the rider may also be usefully confusing the horse into thinking she did want the canter after all. (No correction might mean ▶ 'must have meant she wanted it'.) The same would apply if she accepted a 'wrong' strike-off in schooling and perhaps turned it into a 'correct' lead by crossing the diagonal and working on with it. A mistake or disobedience by the horse has been transformed into useful work – and the horse has been subtly kept under the rider's influence without any conflict. Since there has been no interruption or argument, the message the horse receives is something like: 'Whatever you do is useful: there is no disagreement between us' – and his attentiveness has been reconfirmed.

We can feel when we are in rapport with a horse when he appears to be in rapport with us. A lovely moment of mutual attentiveness – Karen and Billy.

Pacing

These examples bring us to one of the major means of creating rapport in communication: pacing. Pacing is about joining the other where they are – in their map of the world. If we want to give them information, or to influence their behaviour, we have to begin where they are. We cannot expect them to join us – yet often that is what we do. If we bring a sleepy horse out of his stable on a hot afternoon and ask him to do schooling, we are straining our friendship and are likely to get a poor result. If we get angry with him for being excited at a show (the equivalent of a 'party' in our terms) we are not understanding his experience of the world at that time, and only adding conflict to his previously hyped up state. If we bring him out of the stable and ask him to begin taxing work straight away, we are not respecting the state of his muscles any more than in the other examples we were respecting the state of his mind.

Turn the equation around. *If we show rapport by pacing our horse, we allow him to show us rapport in his response to us.* NLP calls this process **pacing and leading**. By starting where our partner in communication is, we are best placed to tell him where we would like him to go.

How can we pace our horses? Here are some ideas. You will be able to think of others.

• Each time you ride, notice what state your horse is in. Ask yourself how you can match that state.

> ■ Perhaps you can groom in rhythm to his breathing (rather like stroking a cat in the same rhythm as its purr). Perhaps you can talk in that rhythm, then speed up so that you help him get energised. Do you ever sing to him?

• Pace the gaits. As you begin your mounted work, use the first few moments or minutes to find out what your horse is offering today. Use your broader knowledge to check out whether a slow walk is the result of stiffness, tiredness, boredom or laziness. We all have lots of additional information to bring to bear, from our previous experiences of other horses as well as of this particular horse.

- Memorise the rhythm and speed of your horse's basic walk, trot and canter, so that you can check against this. How does each gait feel when you replay it in your head? Is today's offering the same, or different? If you ask for more energy, are you still respecting the natural rhythm? Many dressage riders, for example, think they are asking for greater impulsion (energy) when they are in fact telling their horse they want faster movement. It can be helpful, as well as fun, to find a tune that matches each gait. Singing or humming as you ride can help stabilise the rhythm in both of your minds, and will also help you to breathe in a more regular and relaxed way.

- Relate what you do today to the information you are getting from your horse. The next section, on Outcomes, will also help here: as I explain there, a desired outcome-goal – which is outside our control may be doomed to fail. If we take account of the state our horse is in mentally and physically, we can modify our goal for the day realistically, and are thus more likely to be able to achieve it. So rapport is not just a way of building a pleasant relationship with our horse: it's an important element in framing and achieving goals for our riding.

- Is he showing a lack of energy, and might this be a sign of boredom? Might he be tired from doing several days' hard work? Would it be best to reward this and give him some variety by going for a hack? Is what you have in mind likely to repeat what you have been doing for the last few days? His tolerance for repetition is likely to be less great than yours – after all, you know you are working up to a competition but he doesn't! Would it be better to jump rather than do dressage (or flatwork rather than more jumping)? Is he, on the other hand, bursting out of his skin? Would a fast gallop match his mood and use up some of that energy?

- Think about some times when you 'got it right'. How did you know that you got it right?

- What enabled you to do that? List not just your physical behaviour but what and how you were thinking. You might have been thinking in words ('I'm looking forward to gridwork today') or in pictures (seeing yourselves jumping fluently over the fences) or you might have been imagining how it would feel as he rose underneath you with a rounding and swing of his back at each fence.

● Reward wherever you can. Praise confirms. If you can praise your horse, you give him an incentive to offer you even more. If you do not reward acceptable or good behaviour, how is he to know it is what you wanted? With horses as with humans, it is all too easy to 'comment' more on what is not wanted than on what is.

■ Develop a variety of ways of saying 'Yes' to your horse. The word itself. A stroke. A pause and a loose rein. Stopping that exercise as soon as he has done it really well once . After all, you also ask him to repeat something when he hasn't done it properly. How is he to know the difference?

■ List the forms of 'Yes' you already use. Does anyone you know use any others? Could you try one out? At the end of each ride praise yourself for any good communication you have made with your horse. Replay it in your head to make the most of the learning and to reinforce it. It is all too easy to go over and over something we got wrong – what's the message in that? Taking time to repeat enjoyable and successful experiences, and to understand what we did that made them so, lays the foundation for more good experiences.

■ Be kind to yourself about any mistakes. If we concentrate on the failure, we reinforce the bad feelings or simply push the whole experience away because it makes us feel bad. If we use the information as feedback, perhaps with the help of a friend or trainer, we can learn why we got the result we did, and work out what we might need to do to convey a different message – and thus get a different result – another time.

I have given a number of examples of rapport between horse and rider; but this is only one of the relationships in which the rider is involved. We can be in, or out, of rapport with ourselves, and with our trainers. The same basic conditions affect these dialogues too.

Rapport with self

The rider's rapport with self also depends upon a willingness to pace – to begin by accepting one's own starting place. Many human endeavours are clouded by messages of 'ought', 'must' or 'should'. Even if these began as messages from outsiders (parents or teachers, most often) we can continue to repeat them to ourselves with much the same effects. It is important to ask ourselves questions

Develop a variety of ways of saying 'Yes' to your horse. Nikki and Lolly at Hickstead.

like 'do I want to?' 'who says I must/ought/should?' 'how do I feel today?' and to respect the answers. Many talented youngsters dropped out of riding because of pressure to succeed. Pony Club, local shows, affiliation, an increasingly crowded show diary… then ' she discovered boys and gave up'. Once we are able to make choices for ourselves, we can ask what we ride *for*, and respect the answers that come.

This does not mean that we should give up all ambition or discipline and idle about. By being clear about what riding means to us, both in general and on any one occasion, we can respect our needs, our wishes and our body-mind state more fully; and the experiences that we get will be the richer for it. Sometimes, too, we will recognise that where we start is rather a long way from where we want to get to. This may mean we have to override tiredness, for example, to put in some thorough preparatory work before a competition, or seek expert help when we feel we have reached a plateau or a problem in the development of our skills. Recognising and accepting a starting point doesn't mean we have to stop there. It does, however, mean that we will make a deliberate decision – to pursue a strenuous schooling session when we have a heavy cold; to tackle something we find rather daunting; to ride after work because the horse needs the exercise.

And because we have made that decision knowingly, we are less likely to resent the experience.

Trainer's rapport with the rider

The trainer's rapport with the rider needs to resemble the rider's rapport with the horse. De Kunffy said to me that he believed that training should be based on '*them, them, them, without ego*'. Put another way, a trainer's experience should have equipped them with a greater range of information and choices than their pupils have. As he also said, '*I always choose a curriculum where I have something to alter*'. He looks for '*the Achilles' heel of the horse*' in order to find out where training should be directed, and ensures, through the way he describes what is currently happening and how it can be improved, that he stays in rapport with each and every pupil. This is rare and skilled teaching, and it is based on years of experience and deep professional knowledge. But even the most junior and inexperienced trainer can make their training more effective through attending to the principles of the ROSE.

> A rider of fourteen, who had ridden for only a year, had a friend who wanted to learn. Her teacher said that she could borrow a pony and a lunge line and whip and begin teaching her friend to give her an idea of it. The fourte-year-old began her friend's education as she had been taught herself, on the lunge, teaching her exercises with and without stirrups. Her friend enjoyed riding so much that she later decided it was worth spending her pocket-money on regular lessons.
>
> *The teenager modelled the role of riding teacher as she had herself experienced it. She used the same exercises, and because of good observation and memory was able to offer her friend a similar sound basis to the one she had been given. Beyond this, though, her readiness to help her long-term friend meant that she stayed in rapport. They talked the same language.*

As teachers, whether in a formal or informal capacity, we need to maintain rapport with our pupils and pace their starting state and that of their horse. As pupils, we need to remember that we have the right to say if we don't understand, or if we need more information. Our thoughts are not transparent. Our muscles may not be able to respond to our trainer's instructions as we would wish: perhaps he or she can find another way of explaining which will enable them to do so. Good teachers of riding, as of everything else, develop a flexibility in their language and strategies which allows them to pace their clients with greater facility, and so to lead them more easily. In order to pace, whether it is another person or an animal, we rely on our ability to imagine what it is like to be them. We use what we know in order to estimate more accurately what we cannot ever know, which is the interior of another creature's experience: in other words, we take second position. If we can remind ourselves that whatever comes back to us is feedback we can use, we can think about its possible meanings and about alternative messages we might give, rather as a scientist might reflect on the results of an experiment. The word 'science' means 'knowledge'. In seeking knowledge about what results from our behaviour, we become scientific students in a position to redesign our own experience, and that of those with whom we interact, for the better.

Outcomes

One of the essential bases of good communication is knowing what you want. NLP calls this 'having a well-formed outcome'. In riding as in other areas of life, having a well-formed outcome means that we stand a much greater chance of success.

There are six conditions of a well-formed outcome. We need to:

- state it positively

- be specific about what will be seen, heard, felt when it is achieved (sensory experiences)

- be sure that it is within our control to start and maintain the process

- be specific about how, when and with whom it will happen (details of context)

- ensure that it maintains rather than threatens anything positive that we are gaining from our current behaviour

- be clear that its costs (money, time, effort) and how it relates to our sense of self are all acceptable.

Stating desired outcomes positively

It is very easy to say what we don't want. 'I wish my horse wouldn't keep taking off with me'; 'I don't want to panic before shows'; 'I want to stop him leaning on the forehand'. The reason why this way of putting things is not helpful to us is that the mind doesn't understand negatives. In order to cancel something, it first has to think of it! This means – in terms of what we now know about the way the body and mind interconnect – that the unwanted thought will be also present in the muscles. So we will have called an idea into being in order to cancel it out. Doesn't make sense, does it?

So, what *do* we want? This can take some formulating.

When I took up riding again after a twenty-five year gap, I felt very nervous every time I rode. I used my self-hypnotic skills to ask my unconscious to help me 'relax when I am riding'. No joy. What was wrong with my request?

After a while, when my trainer unexpectedly asked me one day to ride a young stallion we had in the yard, it occurred to me that relaxation was not really an appropriate goal. I was going to need muscular tone, and mental alertness. Even out hacking (perhaps especially when out hacking!) I was going to need my wits about me to anticipate and deal with the unexpected (I remembered tearing a thigh muscle years before when a pheasant flew out of the hedge right in front of my horse and he leapt sideways). So what would be a better way to describe what I wanted? I settled for 'enjoy my riding'. Later, I refined this further, as a wish to 'find a way to enjoy my riding, whatever happens'. 'Find a way' respects the unconscious effort that might be involved – but also presupposes that there will be a way. 'Whatever happens' takes care of most kinds of everyday unexpected events . Stating the goal this way made it much more achievable.

Goals can be short- or long-term; broad or highly specific; but all need to be stated positively.

 ▪ List some short- and long-term goals you have for your riding. Check that they are stated positively. Rephrase them if necessary.

Specifying sensory evidence

This really allows you to provide answers to the question 'how will you know?' And by 'how', is meant 'what evidence will tell you?' If your goal is that your horse will be going better, ask yourself exactly what 'better' means.

What you are searching for here is what will be evident, to you or to an observer, when your goal is achieved. Sometimes these forms of evidence are different. An observer might *see* an acceptable canter transition even though the rider might be *feeling* a slight stiffening. You can rightly be satisfied with an improvement on last time, while still knowing that there is room to achieve more.

In fact, this is an important opportunity for reward for both you and the horse, while retaining an ultimate goal that is still further on. Usually, the gap between *what is* and what we want is too great, and this can make us uncertain or even lose confidence that we can ever achieve it. NLP has a good strategy for dealing with this: it is called **chunking down**. In other words, we break the larger goal down into smaller pieces which we can deal with one at a time. It is really important for us to do this in all our training, since it allows us to relate the immediate to the long-term and to be *successful in terms of both*.

Take a piece of paper and lay it crossways (landscape format) in front of you. Put three headings at the top like this:

1. present state   **3. midway state**   **2. desired state**

1. Under 'present state' write how things are at the moment (that is, what you want to change).

2. Under 'desired state' write what you want to achieve.

3. Ask yourself what would be happening if you were halfway to your goal.

Be as specific as you can about what would actually be happening in each state – and about any feelings that might also be involved.

It is very likely that the gaps between these chunk sizes are still too large, so next:

4. Add in a state which is halfway between the present state and your halfway state. What will be happening then? Be specific.

5. Finally, add a state halfway between the original halfway and your 'desired state'. What will be happening then?

By now you will have detailed descriptions of five stages in a process that can take you from here to there – from how it is now to how you want it to be. Each stage will be a move on from the previous stage, and by listing in detail exactly what will be happening externally and internally you have given yourself a set of mini-goals to work for. You have broken your original goal down into stages.

In the best Blue Peter tradition, here is one I made earlier, concerning my relationship with Vals. At the time I did this, we were hitting something of an impasse in our work together. His concentration was patchy; he was often stiff in the back and not giving to the rein. I was anxious and tense, and not confident in my contact.

1 present state	**3 midway state**	**2 desired state**
Fair rapport occasionally lost	Mutual understanding and respect	High quality mutual rapport
Anxiety (W)	More confident (W)	Mutual enjoyment
Confusion (V)	More attentive (V)	Contact feels like 'holding hands'

Then I added

4 next step	**5 penultimate stage**
More consistent rapport beginning to 'listen' to each other (both)	Building excitement and enjoyment

Having put down what I needed to achieve at each stage, I then added specific details about how he and I would need to be behaving (sensory evidence).

Clearly, your specifics will depend upon your goal; but listing not just *what* you want but *how* you will know when you have got it allows you to measure your success. By listing a number of items, you also give yourself a range of ways to succeed. You can legitimately praise yourselves for achievement in one area while knowing there is more to do in another. In turn, this allows both of you some praise, improves your confidence and puts you both in a better overall state to continue.

Ensuring continual control of the process

This condition, of ensuring that it is within your control to start and maintain the process, is both simple and easily forgotten. The rider's outcome may be to win a class. The horse may be talented, the preparation good, the rider's performance excellent on the day. But what if there is someone there with a better horse, greater riding skill…? Winning cannot be what NLP calls a 'well-formed outcome' because it is not within our control. Modifying the goal to 'doing the best round/test/show we can', however, makes it within our control and therefore well-formed. Again, it also increases our chances of success.

Despite their differences, both riders may have talented horses; both may have prepared well; both may ride excellently on the day. Winning cannot be a well-formed outcome.

A rider told me about 'the best test' she and her horse had done. He had been very distracted and difficult in working in, and she had almost decided to go home. However, he calmed down just before the first test she had entered, and produced a reasonable performance. During the second test he really concentrated and offered some round and balanced lengthened strides across the diagonal. While he was not placed, as there were better horses in the competition, his rider came away feeling delighted with what they had been able to do together.

The rider knew that this horse was not a 'natural' at dressage, and the working-in session had been frustrating and disappointing. However, she and her horse did manage to improve their partnership on the day, and she knew they had done the very best they could. By having a realistic goal, she increased her chances of a real success.

■ Look at your list of goals. Are they ones which are fully within your control, or do they depend on others or upon chance? If so, can you modify them so that they do come within your control?

Being specific about context

Let's take an imaginary goal: 'I want everyone to admire my riding' (well, why not?). Who is 'everyone'? Friends; family; strangers at a show; the international selectors? If you don't know, how will you know when your goal has been achieved?

'I'd like my trainer to praise my work' is much more specific, and achievable.

'I'd like my horse to be more obedient.' If you have identified how you will be able to measure obedience in terms of what your senses tell you (for example, walks home rather than jogging, pulls up when asked politely) you may now need only to add some more detail. In the case of these examples, it might be that the horse already behaved acceptably when alone but not in company (or vice versa), and that you would like him to listen to your aids on both sorts of occasion.

'I'd like to be able to do an accurate, fluent test.' Will it be enough for you to do it at home? Do you have to have an audience, or will it be enough just to know that you did it? Or does it have to be in a competition?

The importance of dotting the 'i's and crossing the 't's like this is again that *you increase your chances of success.*

■ Take your most immediate (short-term) riding goal (for example, *improve our half-halts*) and add specific details to it. Half-halts? Where? When? For what purpose? What will you see, hear, feel, that tells you that you are achieving it?

■ In your own time, do the same for longer-term goals (for example, *gain over 50% in three dressage tests; or, learn how to do flying changes*). Some people may find it easier than others to add fine detail at this time. Review what you have written periodically, see what else can then be added. You can also refer to Chapter Eleven for other helpful skills and strategies.

Ensuring that new goals maintain rather than threaten current positives

This condition can often seem paradoxical at first. What could be positive about being held back by some limitation or lack of achievement? Sometimes there are unconscious benefits to be gained from the current state of things, and so change can feel threatening and be blocked, even though reason tells us it's a good idea. This is one reason why sometimes no amount of talking to ourselves, bullying or even encouraging ourselves consciously will work.

■ Imagine for a moment that every feeling and behaviour, however strange, limiting or bizarre, has a good reason. Think like a detective. Ask yourself what the reason for this particular behaviour might possibly be. You might find it helpful to work with a friend on this, as it can sometimes be easier to be in just one role rather than detective and subject at once!

Let's take a couple of examples:

A rider had always wanted to be able to ride advanced dressage movements. She was persistent, practised at home and had frequent lessons. She wanted to be able to compete, but felt nervous each time and did less well than she did at home. She was irritated with herself, and sometimes felt she was no good.

Another rider, with a similar desire to ride dressage well to a high level, avoided competing. She told herself and others that she didn't have time to compete, but felt that there was somehow more to it than that.

A good question to ask is: '*What does this behaviour/feeling/limitation* **achieve** *for me?*' It may be necessary to ask this question several times, ('*and what does* **that** *achieve for me?*') as each question often reveals another layer of meaning. You will find that there comes a point after several questions where the answers stop coming: it is as though you, or the person you are questioning, have reached the most important answer. Usually, it is quite clear that there is nowhere further to go. It is also then very obvious why you or they were stuck with the limiting behaviour – there was an important, and deeply positive or protective reason for it.

To return to the riders:

> When asked what failing to achieve her best in competitions did for her, the first rider eventually said: 'It stops me standing out'. 'And what does that achieve for you?' 'It stops me rocking the boat.' 'And what does that achieve for you?' 'It means my sister and I stay friends.'
>
> The second rider had rather different reasons. 'I haven't time,' led onto 'It means I don't have to put myself under pressure,' and then to 'It means I can just enjoy my riding as leisure rather than having to feel it is like work.'
>
> *Clearly, in both cases there were important, and personally valid, reasons for the lack of progress or achievement.*

What, then, is the way forward? Or are we to be stuck forever with such blocks? The way forward lies in detaching the positive intention from the particular behaviour which we have been using (usually unconsciously) to achieve it. The first rider's issues were about maintaining a good relationship with her sister. She realised that while it was important for them to avoid competition when they were children, for her to be successful in dressage as an adult might not threaten their relationship at all! The unconscious programme was outdated and irrelevant. However, if she had still felt that competition was an issue between them, she might have been able to find other ways to deal with it more directly rather than by limiting her own achievements. Knowing the positive intention of the behaviour is the beginning of finding ways forward.

For the second rider, the answers opened up other possibilities. She might decide that she still wishes to avoid competition, but now knows the real reason (and this is likely to make her feel that she has *chosen* not to enter rather than that she has *avoided* it). Or, she might explore ways in which she could change her attitude towards competition.

We cannot override the deeply protective functioning of the unconscious, nor need we attempt to once we know what it is trying to achieve for us. Respecting these deep processes is a way of respecting ourselves, and once we separate the aim from the specific ways through which it is sometimes enacted, it is usually much easier to find ways forward. How we are as riders is part of how we are as a whole person. In tackling issues which come up in our riding we may well find we are discovering solutions which affect much broader areas of our lives.

- With or without outside help, follow the thread of positive intentions for one of your 'problem' behaviours until you find its fundamental source. Then ask yourself how you can separate the intention from the behaviour and how you can achieve the intention in other ways.

Being clear that the costs of goals are acceptable

NLP calls this an **ecology check**, and it is a fundamental step before making changes of any kind. In carrying out the check, we can refer to both conscious and unconscious parts of ourselves. We can consciously think through the implications of a planned or desired change; but we can also ask ourselves how we *feel* about it. Unconscious information is expressed very clearly in the body (this is the body-mind connection at work). If we tune in/get in touch – or in that marvellously overlapping phrase '*see how we feel*' – there will be a response that tells us. Perhaps a 'gut feeling' of tension or excitement, perhaps a slight hesitation or reservation. Perhaps a sense of lightening, expansion, or energy surge at the very idea of whatever we are proposing.

A rider has an elderly but still fit horse. He knows that he will not be able to afford to buy another when the first one needs to retire, and is wondering whether to buy a foal or yearling, which he could afford, so that it would be ready to school when the first one stops work.

The costs in this case are partly financial: the outlay doesn't stop with the purchase price. Even a foal needs food and grazing, wormers, injections, foot care, insurance and, importantly, attention. Is the rider able, and willing, to invest both the extra money and the extra time?

A rider's young horse turns out to be rather good at jumping. She tries a few local shows and has some successes. It seems to make sense to affiliate and compete more seriously. Meanwhile, her husband is showing signs of restlessness at trailing around to shows after her. She is having a brilliant time – but is he? Will they weather this extra commitment on her part, or might it put an undue strain on the marriage?

The costs here are largely emotional. There is a horsy sweatshirt with the slogan 'If it's a choice between my husband and my horse, it's the horse every time'. The important issue is being aware of what the possible costs of your desired outcome might be, so that you can ensure that an outcome in this part of your life doesn't conflict with others which are important to you.

A rider finds that her young horse is becoming disobedient and 'pushy'. While she is unhappy about this, she cannot bring herself to 'sort him out' as she loves him greatly and wants to have a good relationship with him, and fears he will dislike her if she 'tells him off all the time'.

We have a somewhat parental role (a mixture of trainer and herd leader, perhaps) in relation to our horses, and this rider's difficulty is rather like that experienced by some parents. It may be rooted in a conflict between short-term goals (peace and good feelings) and long-term ones (discipline and good behaviour), or between a more fundamental confusion in the rider/parent between the wish for a 'good relationship' and the need for clarity and firmness about boundaries.

Again, some separation between goals and behaviour may help here. In the long term, clarity about what is acceptable and what is not is a way of establishing respect, and will save the rider from having to get really heavy or punish her horse later for behaviour which she has actually permitted him to develop. The rider needs to look not only at her behaviour but at what she believes good training and ownership involve.

Look at the broader ecology of your desired outcomes. The more closely they fit with other things which are important to you, the more well-formed they are and the more likely you are to have the commitment to achieve them.

Sensory Acuity

We all possess sensory acuity already, but we may not be aware of exercising it, or know how we can develop it further. Children, who are busy trying to understand the world, are brilliant observers, and will often be stunningly accurate in noticing the behaviour and expressions of people around them. Their ability to interpret what they see may be limited because of the limited range of their social experience and their understanding, but the quality of their attention means that they rarely miss significant items. Indeed, the very fact that their social understanding is not yet very developed means that they usually pay attention to things *as if for the first time*, whereas adults will often make assumptions based on a greater wealth of past experience. Assumptions are the death of true sensory acuity, because they filter it and lead us to distort the evidence actually present.

So, one of the important keys to sensory acuity is to pay attention to all the detailed sensory information available to us, and to ask questions of ourselves which provide yet more information. We can use any or all of our senses to do this.

There is no right way to process experience. Every sense has its ways of enriching us. If we know how we do what we do, we can change our thinking much more easily if we want to. We can also enrich our internal world by adding information from our less favoured senses – for example, by reminding ourselves that sound might be part of the remembered or imagined experience, or asking ourselves what was happening in our body when our eyes were registering something.

> A young rider had a pony which had been quite badly injured in the field and needed veterinary treatment and box rest. Her mother commented after several days that he still looked quite unwell – should they call the vet again? 'No,' the daughter replied, 'He's begun to get better.' 'How do you know that? He doesn't look any different.' 'He smells different.'

> *This young owner has great sensory acuity, and spends a lot of time with her ponies. Although she may not previously have been aware of it, she had in fact registered how that particular pony normally smelt, how this had changed when he was injured, and so she had been able to register a change back towards his healthy smell.*

I have given this example first because it is rather uncommon. However, we do all notice how our individual horses smell, even if we don't notice that we do! Some friends and I – all owners of more than one horse each – were talking about this while we were all in a box with one horse looking at an injury he had received in the field. We sniffed his coat in turn, and all realised we could tell that his individual smell was different from the smells of the other horses we knew. Two of us also had cats, and commented on how we could tell our individual cats from each other by their smell as well as by visible differences. One of the basic methods that we use is contrastive analysis: my grey cat smells more perfumed than my ginger one. My tortoiseshell cat has more shiny fur, my ginger one rougher, thicker fur, my grey one fine 'expensive' fur.

If we want to improve our riding, or our horse's performance, we need to establish a detailed baseline of how things are *now* so that we can assess what changes we wish to make, and evaluate our success at making them. De Kunffy's baseline for assessing his pupils is 'how the Greats did it'. In his case, this in itself is made up of many visual references, and we might usefully break it down into its possible components:

The way of going –
a correct walk
a correct trot
a correct canter.

Each of these will have –
a correct 'working' gait
a correct collected gait
a correct medium gait
a correct extended gait.

The 'correct' picture will also be affected by whether the horse is –
a young, recently backed horse
a novice horse
an advanced horse.

In judging, one needs to have clear mental pictures of good work at the different levels: what does a collected trot at Elementary level look like – and how is that different from one at Advanced or Grand Prix?

While it may sound daunting to think of having to develop such an extensive internal 'reference library' – remember that you already have one! It can certainly be sorted and catalogued, you can add more items to it, you can get quicker at finding the item you want.

■ Think back to when you first learnt to ride (or when you first began to learn your chosen discipline within riding). You are likely to remember some confusions or sense of being overwhelmed by how much there was to know. Now consider some of your current skill and information. How did that difference come about? If you are now wanting to learn even more, how did you come to know that there was more to learn?

*Clear mental pictures of
work at the different levels.
A collected trot at Elementary
level and Grand Prix.*

We can build our picture library by many means: reading books, watching skilled riders in training and performance; watching videos and television. We can ask questions of others in order to catalogue significant items: dressage judges, for example, learn to look for the 'V' shape in a good walk, for the way a soft horse's movement is transmitted via rhythmic pulses in the neck, where less movement is seen in a stiff one. The age-old habit of learning by 'sitting by Nellie' has its roots here: if you watch good performance while at the same time listening to an expert commentary, you learn how to judge and label what you see correctly and with increasing skill. If you are in a position to ask your mentor questions ('What specifically makes you think that is "not forward enough"?') you can then refine your learning still further.

■ Take an example of a skill in your discipline. Check your internal reference library for examples and refinements. Make a note of further information you need or questions you could ask next time you see this skill being demonstrated. What do you want to look out for?

Backtracking is an interesting concept. Television is not the only medium to offer instant replay! We can use all the video controls in our heads to enhance our own visual skills – including pause, rewind, fast forward, voice over and even delete.

When we are watching the Greats, we are of course outside them watching through our own eyes. When we ride, we are watching the world from inside our own eyes. NLP describes this as '**being associated**', because we are strongly connected to the experience. However, as the next section explores in more detail, we can also have a **dissociated** view, where we are watching ourselves as if from outside (like watching ourselves featuring in a film or video). This viewpoint separates us to an extent from our experience – we feel it less strongly. Dissociating can be very helpful for enhancing visual acuity. If your teacher tells you that you habitually look down when riding towards a fence, or when riding dressage, rather than looking straight ahead, try looking at yourself from your trainer's viewpoint, or from that of a family member or friend watching you. When I interviewed Charles de Kunffy, for example, he was somewhat surprised to realise that when he rode competitively he used to watch himself, using a dissociated view to monitor his own performance. Even as he rode he was also watching himself.

A dressage rider I know views herself from a dissociated position in her head while she is riding lateral work, so that she can check the correctness and consistency of the movement. She finds it most effective to imagine she is watching herself from above, so that she can monitor the angle and placing of the horse correctly.

Using a dissociated view, particularly while we are actually doing something, may sound a little strange; but in fact we often do it in ordinary life – for example, when we imagine how good we will look in a new outfit, or how we may 'seem a perfect fool' to others observing us in some tricky or embarrassing situation. For a few moments, we have created a dissociated picture or movie alongside the associated one we are already running. Sometimes this dissociated picture can be helpful, as in the case of the attractive outfit; sometimes unhelpful, as feelings of embarrassment can be made even worse by imagining how others may see us.

Watching herself from above to monitor the angle and correct placing of the horse.

The same is true in riding: if we can use a dissociated picture in a neutral or positive way – to add a means of monitoring to our lateral work, for example, or to see what a splendid picture we and our smartly-turned out and well-behaved partner will be making – then it can be immensely helpful. But if we start 'watching' a problem we are having as if we were a critical audience it usually makes things much worse. If we learn to catch ourselves at it when we start to run an unhelpful dissociated mental video, we can do something more constructive.

■ Take an example of something you do often. It need not be to do with riding, and it could be quite simple and everyday such as washing up or cleaning your teeth. View it first from inside (associated) then from outside (dissociated). Gradually practise changing viewpoint with more complex activities. You could then experiment with running two viewpoints at once – side-by-side, perhaps. One might be associated, one dissociated, or you could have two different dissociated views (a side-view and an overhead one). In which of your riding aims or difficulties might you find this useful?

Half-pass – split screen viewing. Experiment with running two viewpoints side-by-side.

Another widely favoured representational system processes information we get from physical or **kinesthetic** experience. Many people who say they 'aren't imaginative' think they are limited because they don't easily make pictures in their heads, but they may be very 'in touch with' themselves nonetheless. Since riding is a physical activity, it might be assumed that people who do it will mostly be kinesthetic, but riders can represent things visually to themselves just as much as other groups of people, and may be over-reliant upon what they see to inform them about how their horse is going.

The process of selecting information from among the millions of possibilities available at any moment is natural and inevitable. Recognising how we usually go about noticing and processing the world and then extending and refining our range enriches us and gives us more choices in many areas of our lives.

Visual acuity, built on contrasting a number of similar but different images, obviously helps trainers and judges; but it can help riders, too, especially if they get help from watchers on the ground telling them what their actions look like. We can then add this information to what we experience kinesthetically – what it feels like – in an NLP process called **sensory overlap**. If I *feel* energy coming through to me from my horse's hind legs and back as he powers off in lengthened strides, and a knowledgeable watcher says:'He's really got his hocks under him', or 'Now he's engaged', I can use their *visual* feedback to enrich my experience. I can now tell from feel what the correct work is like and at the same time have a picture of it in my head. It's like the difference between silent movies and talkies – there's a whole extra dimension of meaning available.

> I had been watching one rider working, and commented that my only criticism, from a judge's viewpoint, was that she did not bend her pony sufficiently around the inside leg as they went through the corners. As she had not had formal dressage training, she had not heard this comment before. She 'went inside' for a few moments to 'see how it would feel' – and I could see her body making the kind of adjustments it would need to make in riding a better corner. When I met her a few days later she had just won a national Preliminary qualifier, and the judge had commented on the sheet how well the corners had been ridden!

These processes are literally 'the making' of us, one way or another. Sensory overlap can help us because it enriches internal experience, stacking up its influence on external behaviour. Equally, an overlapped limiting experience can cause major obstacles.

A rider was having great difficulty in 'getting' shoulder-in and shoulder-out. We took her internal experience apart to find out how it was having the confusing effect she was experiencing. She is good at creating pictures, but found it difficult to have a sense of 'an overall picture' because she was flipping about between a view of her trainer riding the movement, a close-up of how her horse's neck looked, a close-up of her trainer's hands and no one fixed viewing position. Sometimes she was viewing her trainer, sometimes she was viewing herself.

The helping strategy here was to ask her first of all to go back to the basics. What should a shoulder-in (or shoulder-out) involve in terms of the anatomy and placing of the horse in relation to the school? We drew diagrams which showed from above the positioning of the horse and the various displacements of the shoulders in different movements. Once she had got clear, structured pictures of the movements from this dissociated position, she could overlay onto them details of aiding and kinesthetic (felt) experience, and could build up externally-viewed moving pictures of her trainer and others riding the movements correctly. She then added pictures of the movements from other angles. Finally, she got inside the experience (associated into it) and rode it herself. Once she had built up the correct understanding of the movement, and her role in producing it, in this internal way she was able to go and do it successfully on her horse.

She needed to build up a clearer internal representation of 'how to' do the movement before she could begin to succeed in doing it herself. With a confused internal representation, her body-mind inevitably produced a confused external attempt.

Working with these two riders shows clearly how training is easiest when it works from within the rider's existing representational preferences. The second rider finds picture-making very easy, and although she can add kinesthetic 'feel' she has to work harder at this. But whatever the favoured internal system(s), they will be the basis from which the physical act of riding comes. If you reach the internal system, you reach the rider's mind – and thus influence what their mind enacts through their body.

The third of our most-used representational systems is hearing (**auditory**). To begin with, the importance of this may seem less; but as I have outlined earlier in the book it is in fact essential for monitoring rhythm, that fundamental key to correct action in any gait. Of course we can feel the rhythm of our horse's movements, but we can also hear his footfalls and his breathing. Since a relaxed horse breathes with each stride, the two are indissolubly linked. And if a horse is not relaxed, the mismatch between his strides and his breathing will be a way of letting us know. When the rhythm of the breathing and the gait come together again it will tell us that he has now relaxed again.

This can help us in a number of ways. In the first place, we can listen out for the sound of footfalls to check regularity. This is often surprisingly variable, and becoming attuned to the difference between what we actually hear and a regular, imagined beat in our heads can be a major help in diagnosing degrees of impulsion, engagement, straightness, and also unlevelness or lameness. We are contrasting what we can hear through our ears (hoofbeats) with what we expect to hear in our heads (rhythm). Irregular beats should alert us to the need for further investigation. Beyond this, we can ask about the quality of the sound. If we regularly work on the same surface, we can learn to hear a crisp, clear footfall and distinguish it from a dragging or scuffing one. Dragging ones usually mean a lack of engagement or impulsion.

> Also, take the case of the rider who 'forgets to breathe' when she is concentrating. At home, this means she needs to pause during lessons to get her breath back. In tests, she may 'run out of puff' to the point where she hasn't enough energy left to complete the test to the best of her ability, or to do a second test.

> *Trainers often suggest that riders sing or hum as they ride, because in a very natural way this makes them go on breathing! The rhythm also helps the horse to maintain his rhythm. I suggested that this rider find a tune for each of the gaits which matched the natural rhythm of her horse.*

It is important that you match your horse, because if your tune is faster or slower than his natural in-built rhythm you will **mismatch** him and cause irregularities or tensions. Once the rider just mentioned has practised riding each gait while singing or humming the tune, it will be enough for her to hear the tune in her head without vocalising it. The felt rhythm will ensure that she does not 'forget' to breathe, will dictate the rhythm of her breathing, and will communicate that rhythm through body-mind energy to her horse, thus subtly ensuring he remains in rhythm too.

- Use contrastive analysis to establish the differences between your horse's rhythms and those of other horses that you know. While there will be greater differences, for example, between the rhythms of a pony and a large horse, you may find it more taxing to hear the difference between a similarly-sized Warmblood and a Thoroughbred.

- If you can ride alone in an enclosed area, or get a friend to lunge you, ride with your eyes shut so that you can tune into the sound and feel of your horse's natural rhythm in each gait. Memorise it. Then ask him to quicken a little, or allow him to dawdle. Memorise the differences.

- If you are a dressage rider and can observe schooling or competition that involves variations within the gaits (for example, collected, medium and extended trot and canter), listen to the footfalls without looking. You should be able to hear whether the horse is slowing or quickening the beat, or whether he is correctly keeping to the same rhythm while lengthening or shortening the frame and stride-length.

- If you are in a position to observe advanced horses, listen for the lightness or heaviness of their footfalls. Generally, heavy footfalls in medium or extended work mean that the horse is on the forehand. Horses who carry weight correctly on the hind legs, with a light forehand, make less sound.

As these examples show, sensory acuity rests on detailed observation, and on making comparisons. Contrastive analysis is the basis of knowing what it is that you know. It makes assessment (evaluation, judging) possible. It allows us to identify what and where adjustments need to be made. It also enables us to flesh out the sensory detail of our well-formed outcomes. Here are two more exercises to help with this.

- Take a riding skill or technique which you feel competent at, and replay it in your head. Notice as many details as you can of how you represent it to yourself. Would having even more information enrich or enhance the experience even further? How could you get more? Trainers or other 'friends on the ground' may be very helpful here.

- Take a technique which you find harder. Are there confusions or gaps in the way you represent it to yourself? If there are, how can you now clarify the information so that you can make a more precise and helpful representation?

Experimentation

If at first you don't succeed

try, try, try again.

While this saying enshrines the virtues of persistence, it is only valuable if we add to it the qualification:

…but only try again if you do it differently!

If it didn't work the first time, by definition what we did was in some way insufficient to achieve our goal. Having a well-formed outcome, we will have a benchmark against which we can judge what happened (or failed to happen) – a form of contrastive analysis again. In doing so, we can use our developing sensory acuity to sharpen the distinctions we are able to make in order to pinpoint '*the difference that makes a difference*'. I remember de Kunffy on one occasion tracing a problem in the horse's responses back to the rider's stiff ankle. Like him, we can start from the contrast between intent and outcome, home in (zoom in if we are visual) on points of difference and find out the key area in which changes are needed.

In scientific experiments, it is recognised that you only change one variable at a time. Otherwise, you won't know what change made the experiment work. The same is true for us as riders. If the horse is not 'off the leg' you could try any of the following:

• change his food

• ride plenty of transitions to 'sharpen him up'

• wear spurs

• alter the time of day when you school him

• do some jumping or hacking to alleviate possible boredom

• ask a friend or trainer to ride him so you can see if they get on better with him.

Clearly, these varied solutions (and there are probably dozens of others) presuppose different kinds of underlying problem: diet, mental attitude, rider's lack of skill, need for stronger aiding, environment. If you are going to make changes, it is best to try one at a time.

However, we have an important source of information to guide us: the horse. Let's assume that in what he is doing he is telling us something. We know from everyday life amongst family, friends and colleagues that information about how they feel is often given non-verbally. We 'know' a colleague is not enthusiastic about a proposal for reorganising a department. We 'know' that a family member is irritated, even though they are saying nothing. If we are the source of their reluctance or irritation, we are most likely to improve communication if we vary our approach. I have called this 'experimentation' because the word catches the sense of deliberate yet responsive intervention that characterises good communicators. In the field of NLP people who do this are described as having 'behavioural flexibility', because they have a range of approaches at their disposal. They do something different. They don't try, try, try the same thing again.

So, if we have been seeking to build rapport with our horse, we are clear about what we want (we have a well-formed outcome), and we have been sharpening our ability to distinguish between subtler details of what we see, hear and feel from him in our interaction with him, we can take it that whatever he does in response to our requests or instructions is some form of communication. It doesn't 'just happen' that he gets distracted, or falls onto the shoulder, or runs out at a fence. His actions can usefully be taken as having meaning, and sometimes intent. In order to assess what those might be, we need to enter as far as we can into his world, and rethink our response, or our next communication, in terms of its meaning for him.

A horse was hardworking and good-natured, but when his owner first acquired him and began schooling him there were times when he just 'closed down', 'switched off' and rushed through or away from what she asked. She said it was as if he hoped that he could just get through what was happening so that he could get away from some kind of pressure. She felt that before he came to her too much had been asked of him physically and mentally, because it was at times when she asked something new or taxing of him that he switched off in this way.

The solution for this partnership was for the rider to take the training more slowly and reassuringly, with plenty of praise at each stage, allowing her horse plenty of time to get used to things, to make them automatic, before asking him to learn anything else.

Horses are actually not very different from people in this respect. The process of learning usually begins with deliberate (conscious) attention, and only through repetition does the thing learnt become familiar and thus able to be done automatically. This rider successfully varied *the timing and speed* of her horse's teaching to help him learn at a more comfortable – and therefore more successful – rate for him.

> Another horse was being taught to lengthen stride. Eager to please, and seeming delighted with the praise he got, he started doing lengthened strides whenever he came to the long side of the school or started to cross the diagonal.

> *It was important not to stop his pleasure in lengthening by shortening him up again. The trainer suggested that the rider introduce circles and loops after the short side so that the horse would be asked to use his energy for greater engagement, and at the same time be put in a position where he could 'get it right' without taking charge of deciding what was going to happen next.*

In this case, the trainer's flexibility was shown in being able to devise a way of diverting the horse from producing the outcome he wanted (and thought his rider wanted) without in any way punishing him. The experimentation this involved needed to be guided by the rider/trainer's rapport with the horse and by her sensory acuity in relation to her desired outcomes. This illustrates well the interplay between the four elements of the ROSE. In different situations, different ones may predominate, but all will be necessary if effective communication is to take place. Just as a rose is more than its shape, its petals, its scent, its colour, its thorns, its leaves, so good communication is about the relationship between rapport, outcomes, sensory acuity and experimentation.

In making choices about how to experiment, we have to be guided by the other factors. This will enable us rapidly to discard some options (shouting at the horse if he does not respond to the leg, for example), or to look first for other supporting evidence: for example, before changing his diet we would need to consider his behaviour as a whole, the state of his coat, eye, muscles and general physical tone.

We can encourage ourselves to experiment in a number of ways. First and foremost by honestly considering what we understand by a lack of success in any instance. The very idea of 'failure' is likely to connect with such powerful feelings of disappointment and inadequacy that it will profoundly affect the state in which we approach any attempts at improvement. Often, once we have cleared the old, often childlike feelings about 'failure' away and put ourselves in control again by adopting the role of scientist/experimenter, we are able to think of more ways forward.

■ Take a recent example where your outcome was not what you had intended. How did you feel? How do you feel if you now re-label that 'failure' as information or feedback instead?

When we are working to increase our experimental ability, it is helpful to brainstorm for lots of solutions. This in turn helps us stretch our capacity to become creative problem-solvers. Brainstorming means that we separate the process of generating ideas from the process of evaluating them. It also means that we do not stop as soon as we have found one idea that looks likely to work. We can help build a reference library, or vocabulary, of possible strategies collected from our own experience, that of our friends, anecdotes about others in the horse world, books, videos and lectures. Bearing in mind that we are concerned with communication, we should be prepared to consider behaviours that are effective between people to see if they can be translated into person-horse communication.

If we look at it like this, there is no longer such a clear distinction between strategies directed at skill training/outcomes and those directed at respect/rapport outcomes as there may once have seemed to be. From a horse's stand-point, picking his feet up quickly and willingly when asked is just as much skill learning as recognising the signals for piaffe. Both also involve attention, understanding the meaning of the communication and responding to it. Both involve the rider in conveying the intended meaning clearly and respectfully, and in rewarding/reinforcing it with praise or a quiet 'thank you'. Even for a routine obedience, it is important to let the horse know that we appreciate what he has done.

Having brainstormed a number of possible strategies or techniques that might help us achieve our outcome more fully, we can evaluate their likely effectiveness through the sieve of imagining how the horse will understand them. Usually, the most successful strategies organise things in such a way that the desired behaviour is the most natural response. A good example would be the common way of starting teaching the canter aid by encouraging a transition while giving the aid on a corner, where the horse's balance naturally inclines him to the correct lead. More complex aims, however, may be approached in a number of ways. A horse can be asked for more engagement in the hind legs by

- frequent transitions

- increased use of the rider's inside leg

- lots of turns and circles

- shoulder-in and travers

- slower tempo with increased energy.

De Kunffy's book *Training Strategies for Dressage Riders* shows clearly how schooling can combine many patterns to achieve specific training goals while, at the same time, providing variety and a flow of energetic and enjoyable riding for both horse and rider. Schooling need not be like school!

Schooling need not take place *in* the school, either. As a student, riding in the country during university vacations, I helped school a young heavyweight horse who had been bred at a nearby farm. My parents' house was on a lane, which led past the farm entrance and then became a track winding for about a mile between fields. I remember teaching Silver Queen how to respond to leg aids by moving her from side to side across the track while setting off for our hacks. I also helped her learn to balance herself on turns by riding corners in a rather small but tidily rectangular field.

If we are in good rapport with our partner, have a clear idea of our intent, and are paying attention to sensory information and feedback, we can seize natural and unexpected opportunities that offer themselves. If we remember that every act is understood as a communication of some sort, we can ensure that the meaning of many more of our actions around our horse will be consistent with what we would want him to understand. Being with each other can then truly be 'roses all the way'.

CHAPTER 5

He Didn't do it – Specific Communication Difficulties

Basically, there may be four reasons why a horse does not do what the rider
has in mind: the rider's aid was not understood; the horse was not physically
or mentally ready to comply with the rider's wishes; a sufficiently advanced
horse, receiving correct aids, wilfully disobeys them; or the horse evades
the rider's influence by playfulness.

CHARLES DE KUNFFY *Training Strategies for Dressage Riders*

If another person is involved in your outcome, the objective is to
overlap that person's outcome with yours to produce a 'heads I win,
heads you win' solution. This is dovetailing outcomes.

GENIE Z LABORDE *Influencing with Integrity*

Respect between horse and rider must be mutual: in that
sense, we surrender to him too.

CHARLES DE KUNFFY *The Ethics and Passions of Dressage*

'He didn't do what I wanted!' The rider's complaint may be spoken or
silent, an accusation or an admission. But we have all experienced the
disappointment and frustration which it expresses. In this chapter I
shall draw on NLP in looking at the horse's non-compliance from a new angle:
what does it tell us about the horse's experience of our intentions and our
aiding, and how, bearing this in mind, can we so orchestrate our own behaviour
that 'submission' becomes not a slavish or fearful yielding but a willing,
enabling, mutually enhancing experience? In particular, I shall look at some
specific problems of communication between horse and rider: disobedience,
evasion and anticipation.

The very words themselves give us clues as to our own expectations and beliefs: *disobedience* implies that there is a rider request or command to be obeyed; *evasion* implies that the horse understands something and intentionally or deliberately chooses to do something else instead; *anticipation* again implies an understanding on the horse's part, and, further, that the horse acts, before receiving an instruction, upon his assumption of what is wanted – producing an action which may or may not be what the rider actually wanted.

There are fundamental assumptions here about the degree to which the horse understands the rider's requests but opposes them on the basis of intentions of his or her own. In teasing out the implications of these ideas from the NLP viewpoint of what is communicated, and how, I shall draw extensively upon an interview I had with Charles de Kunffy. His wealth of experience in riding and in training horses and riders combines with the new understanding which NLP gives us. This combination offers us an approach to the concepts of aiding and submission which works because it is based upon the principles of good communication, and entails the building of an ever more refined dialogue between horse and rider, rider and horse.

I should like to begin with an example of my own. Quite coincidentally, the day before writing this chapter I rode our eighteen-year-old schoolmaster, Lolly, for the first time for months (my husband Leo usually rides him). It felt good to be able to play with him, whereas if I had been riding Vals, our younger horse, I would have felt more responsible for using the session as schooling. In NLP terms, riding Lolly cues me into a recreational state, whereas riding Vals cues me into a working/teaching state. (And no doubt the differences are communicated to them in the way I ride.) It was a cold, sunny, winter day. I had no particular agenda, except to exercise Lolly and myself and to rediscover what we could do together. Feeling rather stiff from digging out the edges of the sand school the day before, I did more walk and canter than trot. In terms of its content, our session included walk to canter transitions, leg yields, shoulder-in, a little half-pass, some walk pirouettes, circles of various dimensions, some serpentines, some attempts at halt to canter. But the experience of the session was something else again. From the first moment I got on, Lolly was there for me: attentive, immediately volunteering himself on the bit, walking with energy, trotting with lift and rhythm, cantering with real collection and suspension entirely on the seat. We had the kind of contact I dream of: minimal yet responsive. Lolly never has a wet mouth – yet this time it was soft with a real 'moustache'. It was a very special ride. I could not have asked for a better experience of mutual attentiveness, respect and enjoyment. And it reaffirmed my belief that such experiences are possible if we care enough about creating the relationship and endeavouring to make our intentions clear to our partner.

Yet Lolly is by no means a doddle. Like many schoolmasters, he can be stubborn and offer as little to his rider as he thinks he can get away with. His sway back and long neck make it easy for him to evade the contact and drop below or behind the contact. He knows the evasions of crookedness too. In the past we have had many battles with him – doomed to be fruitless, as I now believe, because they were based on unhelpful beliefs – that he was inherently lazy and stubborn; that horses generally want to do as little work as possible; that it is the rider's job to be the boss and 'tell' the horse, or to 'sort him out' if he doesn't do what he is asked. If these things were true, yesterday's experience could not have happened. While, no doubt, my riding has improved considerably in the eight years we have had Lolly, the submission and attentiveness he gave was *offered*, not demanded. For that half hour or so, we were in a genuine dance of mutual communication and mutual pleasure. And this brings me to the first major issue of this chapter, that of belief.

Lolly was there for me…

Beliefs and Their Effects

NLP shows us that of all the areas of our experience, our beliefs and values come second only to identity in terms of their importance to us. As Robert Dilts pointed out:

> Beliefs are not necessarily based upon a logical framework of ideas. They are, instead, notoriously unresponsive to logic. They are not intended to coincide with reality. Since you don't really know what is real, you have to form a belief – a matter of faith.
>
> ROBERT DILTS *Beliefs, Pathways to Health and Well-Being*

Beliefs are, in other words, hypotheses – but we often treat them as if they were facts. However, they are incredibly powerful. Dilts explains one key reason why this is so: 'When you really believe something, you will behave congruently with that belief.'

Thus, belief is unconsciously enacted in behaviour. This is one reason why we get the results we expect. Another, as I explained in an earlier chapter, is that we have to filter the enormous volume of information we get in order to make sense of it, and the filtering processes of distortion, deletion and generalisation are also affected by our beliefs. Thus there are two ways (at least) in which our beliefs become self-confirming.

To return to Lolly, my experiences in learning NLP and in beginning to apply it to horses have changed what I believe about him: I now recognise that his conformation has affected both him and his riders, making it difficult for him to 'round up' – and no doubt he often found it uncomfortable, too; his temperament has ensured that when bullied or commanded he has become evasive, where perhaps another horse would have been cowed and compliant. Knowing him better as an individual, I realise that he is actually quite affectionate and does like to please, provided he is asked nicely. In particular, he wants freedom in his mouth. Over the years, with previous owners as well as us, there have been struggles to 'get him on the bit': I now tend to think that many of these involved riding him 'from front to back' – using the hand to create the shape artificially rather than riding him forward from the leg. At times of desperation, we resorted to the dreaded draw-reins, which do the same thing but with less effort from the rider. The biggest step forward, though, came about a year ago, when we were inspired one day to take off his flash noseband and loosen his cavesson: his immediate response said effectively 'At

last you have realised what I wanted – now I can soften my jaw and flex in my neck.' Our new trust in him immediately inspired a new trust in us, and for the most part a more cooperative and willing horse.

A clear opinion of 'the dreaded draw-reins'.

I have no doubt that the change in my beliefs about him will have been expressed in changes in my behaviour, which will, in turn, have been expressed physically, interacting with his responses to produce the self-fulfilling spiral of a good experience for us both.

We cannot function without beliefs, yet because they are often unrecognised as such they can be difficult to identify and their effects difficult to unpick. In drawing attention to them, and to their 'fictional' quality, NLP makes them more accessible for our examination – and thus brings them within the scope of our control. The question is not which beliefs are more 'true' but which are more *useful*.

In the 1950s a management expert named Douglas McGregor wrote about the effects of two contrasting approaches to management. He named them Theory X and Theory Y. I shall give a fuller description of them here because I believe they can really help us to understand the effects that our beliefs about our horses have on us in our riding.

Theory X

1. The average man is by nature indolent – he works as little as possible.

2. He lacks ambition, dislikes responsibility, prefers to be led.

3. He is inherently self-centred, indifferent to organisational needs.

4. He is by nature resistant to change.

5. He is gullible, not very bright…

The implications for management are:

1. Management is responsible for organising the elements of productive enterprise.

2. With respect to people, this is a process of directing their efforts, motivating them, controlling their actions, modifying their behaviour to fit the needs of the organisation.

3. People must be persuaded, rewarded, punished, controlled, their activities must be directed.

Theory Y

1. People are not by nature passive or resistant to organisational needs. They have become so as a result of experience in organisations.

2. The motivation, the potential for development, the capacity to assume responsibility, the readiness to direct behaviour towards organisational goals, are all present in people. It is a responsibility of management to make it possible for people to reorganise and develop the human characteristics for themselves.

3. Management is responsible for organising the elements of productive enterprise in the interest of economic ends, but their essential task is to arrange the conditions and methods of operation so that people can achieve their own goals best by directing their own efforts towards organisational objectives.

From McGregor, *The Human Side of Enterprise*, 1960
in Charles Handy, *Understanding Organisations*, Penguin 1976

As Handy shows, these contrasting beliefs about the nature of human beings lead to very different beliefs about what kinds of behaviour are needed to manage them. Theory X management is directive and controlling because it rests upon a low estimation of people's inherent motivation (*forwardness*) and willingness to take responsibility (*self-carriage*). Theory Y management rests on the belief that people are inherently motivated, and that management needs to ensure that the conditions in which they work are such as to encourage, not hinder, this. Not that far away from contrasting beliefs about horses, really…

If we believe that horses are idle, unintelligent and stubborn, we are led towards a regime of control – punishment and reward, sticks and carrots. If we believe that horses have the capacity to relate to human beings and to learn to wish to please them, because fulfilling their wishes has become for them a comfort or pleasure in itself, then we are led towards a regime which seeks to create harmony and mutual satisfaction:

> The delight of the great equestrian, however, is the horse's willing submission to his wishes. Born of confidence that the decisions are for pleasure, the horse seeks his rider's guidance. He submits in recognition that our intentions are identical with his needs.

> The instant willingness of the horse to respond to the imperceptible suggestions of a sophisticated rider is the very by-product of years of harmonious familiarity and the resultant attitude of joy to please.
>
> CHARLES DE KUNFFY *The Ethics and Passions of Dressage*

But most of us are not 'great equestrians' or 'sophisticated riders'. Of course not, but we can all respectfully prioritise the experience, needs, feeling and nature of our horse. Our beliefs and attitudes are subtly conveyed to our horses, through our unconscious body language as well as through our deliberate actions. These can, to a considerable extent, compensate for many of our technical limitations. Horses can be incredibly forgiving within the context of a real partnership with their rider. They will accept many variations in aiding, ranging from everyday lack of subtlety and skill to major adaptations necessitated by a rider's actual handicap. I have sometimes judged handicapped riders in affiliated competitions and have been humbled by their skill and by the evident rapport between them and their horses.

It is this mutuality which forms the basis of true submission. Karen and Billy.

It is this mutuality which forms the basis of true submission. In discussion with me, Charles de Kunffy said:

> This concept of submission: the physical submission is simply to submit the haunches for the rider's directions, and to submit the resilience of the back to carry the rider rather than to push him. But the kind of partnership you see between horse and rider in the Spanish Riding School or any good schools… there was a relationship, and you often wonder if the horse has taken the rider and substituted it for the instinctual codes [of flight and fight].

In *The Ethics and Passions of Dressage* he says: 'The rider must offer his mind to guide the body of the horse, while both of their spirits are animated by the joy of this partnership.'

Reasons for Non-compliance

At the beginning of this chapter I quoted the four reasons de Kunffy gives for a horse not doing what the rider wants. Let us now consider these in more detail.

Lack of understanding of the aids

It is clear from de Kunffy's writing and teaching that he believes the responsibility for this is always the rider's. In this, his beliefs accord with the NLP presupposition I discussed earlier, that *the meaning of a communication is the message which is actually received*. Riding recently, I became aware that Lolly was going quarters-in while cantering along the long side of the school. In attempting to straighten him I failed to correct him properly by bringing his shoulders in, thoughtlessly attempting instead to push his quarters out by pressuring him with my inside leg. Not surprisingly, he thought I was asking for a flying change – and obliged with much enthusiasm before 'taking off' in high spirits on what was for me the 'wrong' leg. So far as he was concerned, I was asking for a change – and he obeyed what he understood. (The enthusiasm was his own contribution – again, blameless, because we don't do changes very often and he is excited when he gets it right, as he thought he had this time.) Charles would call this an 'honest mistake'; and as he said to me '*An honest mistake is really a rider mistake – always a rider mistake*'.

'…the message received?' Both parties look as if this is hard work. Nikki and Vals.

The 'voluntary' flying change – some 'honest mistakes'.

Horse not physically or mentally ready

The second type of non-compliance occurs because the horse is not physically or mentally ready to comply – in other words, rider error again, because we are asking too much too soon. We might argue, in terms of training, that there always has to be a first time for a new skill or manoeuvre; but any mistake occurring in these circumstances is definitely one to be accepted without blame or chastisement, or the horse will rapidly learn fear of the movement. A young horse who, on being asked for canter, strikes off on the 'wrong' leg; who cannot sustain his balance and 'falls out' of canter after half a circuit; who loses attention and spooks at a tub of flowers at an early competition: these are faults of inexperience.

Unbalanced and falling out of canter.

In these circumstances we need to be opportunistic: to use the movement which the horse offers, as if we had asked for it, rather than stopping or punishing him. Alternatively, we need to experiment to find ways to 'load' the manoeuvre for success another time: asking for canter on a corner, beginning the canter with a half-halt to start from a better balance; having tubs of flowers at home for the horse to get used to, are all respectful ways to address the problem and get the desired result.

Wilful disobedience

The third reason given for non-compliance is that a horse who is sufficiently advanced and is receiving the correct aid, wilfully disobeys. This raises some interesting questions. When we discussed disobedience, de Kunffy was very clear that *'The horse reacts to what's being done to him. He doesn't have a plan. He doesn't have a goal.'* From this perspective, therefore, it makes sense to look for reasons for disobedience which are meaningful to the horse in terms of his view of the world. It is in theory possible that a horse might 'take on' a rider – but why would he do this? Theory X might argue that this is because he is lazy, argumentative, unmotivated, etc. Theory Y would counter that this puts the responsibility back on the rider to communicate that compliance with the request is somehow in the horse's own interests: the horse needs convincing that what is asked for is more comfortable, easier, just what he really wanted, etc. The responsibility here is on the rider to help the horse to reach this understanding; and in doing this the rider has two allies: aids and schooling patterns.

In *The Ethics and Passions of Dressage* De Kunffy has some thought-provoking things to say about the meaning of 'aiding'.

Aiding is a perpetual, subtle, form of rewarding!…

No creature fails to recognize aid, when it is offered to assist him in doing something better and doing it with less effort…

Aids, being gestures of help, build confidence and induce resultant submission of the horse to the rider's will. This submission is born of trust and verified by harmony.

In conversation, he said: '*When a horse makes a mistake, it is always an honest mistake because he misread something by his trainer or his coach*'. However, we are inclined to confuse the issue by labelling such mistakes 'evasions' or 'disobediences' . In de Kunffy's view, this really just demonstrates that the horse has caused annoyance in the rider! (In psychological terms, we would say that the rider is projecting their own feelings onto the horse.) However, de Kunffy argues that some failures to obey are the result of tension or fear in the horse. '*Fear of being chucked in the mouth, fear of the spur. The only difference is the degree of the reaction*'. In dealing with disobedience of this kind, he said, '*You really have to*

'…tension or fear in the horse'. Leo and Vals. Taken not long after his arrival, this picture shows Vals and Leo sharing some anxiety.

come to the source of the fear, and work with the disobedience as a secondary response to the fear'. And it is likely that some examples of disobedience by a horse who does understand the aid and is capable of performing the movement do relate to pain or fear.

As I explained earlier in the book, Vals has always shown tension about upward canter transitions, tending to hollow and run, and we assume that this dates back to some painful or rough and ready experiences of being broken as a youngster in Russia. What began, probably, as a difficulty of inexperience and immaturity then became a learnt anxiety. In working with him both Charles and other master trainers advocated patience, lack of fuss, tolerance of the hollowing and running and the use of specific patterns which would encourage an easy transition. One suggestion which helped when he was younger was to work him on a small circle with a loose outside rein, encouraging a very deep outline and an exaggerated inside bend, then ask for the transition, so that the outline was soft and there was no danger of the rider accidentally blocking the transition or catching the horse's mouth as he made the first large leap forward into the new gait. What had begun as a problem of physical immaturity had now become one of the mind. Therefore it could only be corrected by methods which respected the original cause of fear and which at the same time addressed the learnt anxiety. This approach resulted in a considerable lessening in anxiety, and much calmer transitions.

Encouraging without blocking.

So the disobedience which demonstrates tension, indicates fear or anxiety. And in such states, the horse activates a different set of muscle groups from those he uses when he is relaxed. The primitive flight/fight impulses not only take his attention away from what the rider is saying, but by activating the 'wrong' muscle groups for supple athletic work actually make it physically impossible for the horse to do what is asked.

> Some while ago, I was judging an Elementary dressage competition in an outdoor arena in winter. The weather was dreadful: slashing heavy rain and wind, so extreme that I had to have my car engine running throughout the competition in order to keep my windscreen wipers moving! Not surprisingly, many horses were unable to concentrate. The wind was causing some advertising banners around the arena to flap; the wet patches on the sand were glinting in a terrifying way; and the rain itself was coming at them from different angles. In these horses, a wholly understandable primitive fear activated their flight/fight muscles: they were tense and hollow, their strides short and irregular, even when they were not actually shying or refusing to go forward. A few horses, however, were not concerned by the weather. They were able to produce calm, rhythmical, soft, rounded work, not just because they were physically skilled or well trained, but also because their lack of anxiety allowed them to use a different set of muscles.

In our conversation, de Kunffy emphasised that, where a horse is tense, the rider's responsibility is to work first with the horse's state of mind. '*The rider should convince the horse that what is asked for is non-threatening, can be done in relaxation and improved balance; and very likely he will do it.*' He summed up this part of our conversation by drawing the distinction between an honest mistake, which the rider should see as an opportunity for further teaching, and a *disobedience* (showing tension), where the appropriate correction is *the elimination of the cause, which is usually fear.*

 ▪ List some recent incidents where your horse has not done what you asked. Examine each of these in the light of this distinction. Was it an honest mistake? Or was it a disobedience caused by tension or fear? How did you respond at the time? Thinking it over in the light of these explanations, how would you respond if it occurred again? Would you make any changes, and if so what and why?

Playfulness

The fourth type of disobedience is that of playfulness by a horse who fully understands and is capable of performing what is asked. In this case, the rider's response needs to be considered in the light of what it tells the horse. If the rider allows the movement (an exuberant buck when asked for a canter transition, for example), will the horse take this as a permission to repeat it? There have been some famous showjumpers who bucked after clearing difficult fences – which, on occasion, lost them valuable time in speed competitions. I remember, however, that the famous Vibart used to wait until after the final fence before bucking. I would, nowadays, be curious to know whether his rider had corrected bucks that occurred earlier in the round but allowed that final, celebratory but also non-compromising one…. As riders, we are always having to make decisions – and sometimes it is great to enjoy a mutual sense of play with our horses. However, we need to be mindful that horses are always learning something by what we do and don't do: as de Kunffy emphasises, no action we make is neutral so far as they are concerned – they learn everything indiscriminately. So perhaps we need to ask ourselves, in that split second before we react (or don't) what message we want our horse to receive about what he just did…

Anticipation

Anticipation may also seem like a kind of disobedience, in that it is an action which is either not asked for, or occurs before the rider asks for it. Since the newer dressage tests often don't have a halt at X, judges now see horses hesitating on entry as they approach the magic spot. Others have to be cajoled past X to complete a final halt at G. No doubt, many of these are older horses, who learnt through long practice that X was where you stopped. Well trained, ready to please, they do it anyway. At higher levels, horses crossing the centre line (as in a serpentine) at canter will often volunteer a flying change, as they will also do at F, K, M or H… That, after all, is where changes happen, isn't it?

Those horses learnt what we allowed them to experience. We didn't mean that the movement should be associated with the place, but if we asked for it often enough at that place the horse, being a creature of habit,

Anticipation. Horse thinks: 'At C, track right. Must be Prelim. 6, 10, 14, 18, Novice 21, 32, 35, 37 or 39 then…'

learnt to associate the two. As riders, we need schooling, too – schooling to keep schooling varied and non-repetitive, so that the horse learns to associate the movement with the request for it, not with external circumstances.

When we discussed anticipation, de Kunffy made an interesting and unexpected point:

> We have to remember, first, that all training is based on anticipation. You cannot train a human or an animal without them eventually detecting your preparation and setup as leading to a familiar scene. A horse has to anticipate a flying change…

> Sometimes we inadvertently set things up and the horse starts to anticipate. Horses have no ability to analyse or synthesise or plan; but they do have excellent memory, and based on this memory is all training.

As he went on to explain, horses have both neuromuscular memory (how to do things) and mental memory (things that feel safe or threatening). The first is what NLP calls the **how to**; and our schooling is largely directed to establishing these neuromuscular skills – lowering the inside hip and taking weight on the inside hind in shoulder-in, for example, or the whole complex set of interrelated physical processes and movements which constitute what we call self-carriage. De Kunffy also made the following points about anticipation:

> Anticipation is in a way welcome, if a horse is correctly trained you want them to habituate posture, movement, balance and traditions of weight-bearing on the haunches… an anticipated way of moving.

> All good training somewhere relies on anticipation; but if there is anxiety and tension that is again fear-based – totally the rider's fault.

> If a horse fears a canter transition or a piaffe and starts to blow up, no way is that instinctive– it is totally acquired behaviour, trainer induced…the trainer strategies have to be changed. Changing the rider's nature so the rider behaviour changes. The horse behaviour will follow.

It may seem that the approach described in this chapter places a heavy responsibility upon the rider, and indeed de Kunffy is very clear that this is so, and very aware that in the way we describe what is going on (reflected also in the marking system for dressage, which gives only one mark to the rider and all the rest to the horse) we *reinforce the falsehood that the mistakes are the horse's by using that language: 'the horse is tense', 'the horse is resistant'... 'out of rhythm' . It should be 'the rider is out of rhythm'.*

De Kunffy is one of the greatest of communicators with horses, both in practice and in his theoretical understanding of what is involved. Like the great communicators whose practice first stimulated the study that became NLP, he recognises that the responsibility for all communication must rest on the partner who initiates it. If we wish to address our horses, it is up to us to do the best we can to make what we have to say to them intelligible, clear, and preferably worth listening to. This is a courtesy we owe them, particularly as they are in a position where they have no choice but to listen to us! But if, at times, this sounds like a great deal to ask of us, we can remind ourselves that along with the responsibility comes choice. And choice can be exciting, freeing and enabling.

In the context of communication, I believe riders have three invaluable guides to help them:

1. What is known and handed down about effective ways of communicating with horses – the great traditions of classical riding.

2. Their personal knowledge of their individual horse.

3. What is increasingly known about the principles of effective communication as such – NLP.

The language of classical riding, refined as it has been through centuries of both essential and artistic communications, gives us a subtle and wide-ranging vocabulary for our conversations together. Our own personal relationship with an individual horse allows us to target what we say and how we say it, according to our individual natures and the relationship between us. And an understanding of how communication itself works, how it can fail to work, and how we can use those apparent 'failures' as information, so that we can succeed in communicating effectively after all, gives us a refined kit of tools that are easily understood and used.

In this light, the mistakes, disobediences and acts of anticipation which occur in the relationship of every rider with every horse can be seen as providing us with valuable information on where we can improve our communication so as to make it even better. Far from disheartening us, these apparent glitches can be a source of fascination and an inspiration to experiment in the search for new solutions. They can also be a source of wonder at the fact that, for so much of the time, we and our horses can successfully manage such an amazing process as communicating with each other at all.

Problems of Muscle and Message

The truly talented riders are recognized as having 'feel', which depends on the talent for being a living antenna that picks up all communication the horse sends. The magic of perception and awareness, supplemented by intelligence, compassion, and empathy, can induce the rider to proper actions. For a knowledgeable observer, this soon becomes apparent. When schooling his horse, the good rider should 'make sense' to an onlooker.

CHARLES DE KUNFFY *Training Strategies for Dressage Riders*

CHAPTER 6

Tuning in – Getting in Touch – Seeing Your Way to it

Harmony has its physical bases. Those riders who have 'feel', that mysterious
and oft-mentioned but seldom explained concept, are well on their way
toward the art of riding. 'Feel' is predominantly an ability to physically seek
harmony through the most accommodating position of togetherness.
CHARLES DE KUNFFY *Training Strategies for Dressage Riders*

You make your map and you have to live in it. Remember two things as you create it:
1. How you use your senses on the outside is going to affect your thinking
and experience on the inside.
2. You can change your experience by changing how you use your senses on the inside.
JOSEPH O'CONNOR AND IAN MCDERMOTT *Principles of NLP*

Riding, on the face of it, is a physical art, but as I hope I have already begun
to show, it is the result of a wonderfully complex set of activities in
both body and mind. The word 'feel' seems to point to a kinesthetic
(body-based) dimension of experience, but we now know that mind and body
are not separable, and so any bodily act has its corresponding mental processing, whether conscious or unconscious. If 'feel' in riding is the ability to seek
harmony with the horse, then in having it as our goal we can, and must, use all
our abilities, mental and physical.

At the beginning of the book, I explained how NLP has shown us that when
we do what we call thinking we are in fact using information from our different
senses (*representational systems*) to do that internal processing. For the most
part, we are using information from sight (visual), bodily sensation (kinesthetic)
and hearing (auditory). For whatever individual reasons, we each tend to have

our own favourite representational systems, and to become experts in their use while relying less, little, or perhaps virtually not much at all, on others.

While we can live adequate, even rich, lives in this way, nonetheless our choices can be limited, and our ability to influence and shape our lives correspondingly restricted. As NLP began to examine questions of communication, it became clear that the people with most influence in any situation were the ones who had the greatest flexibility – in other words, the greatest range of choices available to them. Outstanding people in any sphere will tend to draw upon a rich range of internal processing as well as behavioural strategies.

Since we now know so much more about how we work, and 'what works' in communicating with others, we have the means of developing ourselves. We are not stuck with being people who 'can't visualise' or 'have little feel for things' or 'aren't in tune'. If we know what we lack, and want to add it to our range, we can begin to do it. And so we can all improve our 'feel' in the fullest sense.

In Chapter One, Working from the Inside, I explained how the language we use can give clues to which representational systems we prefer. So the first stage of enriching ourselves is to identify which system(s) are our natural favourites. After this, we can decide which other systems we want to use more, to build up a richer experience that will make us more effective. Then, we can go about this in two ways: by deliberately exercising ourselves in our less-practised systems, and by modelling other people who naturally use them easily. The end result is to develop our ability to build harmony with our horse – creating that 'togetherness' which, however intermittent, is still the most precious experience for both horse and rider.

It is important to recognise a paradox here: as in human relationships, even an excellent relationship is not experienced as ecstatic all the time! There are mundane times, sometimes moments of routine, confusion, difference or even boredom; but the baseline can still be one of mutual respect and attentiveness. So it is in our relationship with our horses. The greatest moments are by their nature ephemeral: a great hack, a wonderful test, a few steps of perfect piaffe. These outstanding moments are not the benchmarks by which we measure a good partnership, or excellent riding, or a well-trained horse. They are the peaks of the relationship. The benchmarks are both more everyday and more attainable.

Even if your horse will never reach Grand Prix, he can still be a true dressage horse. As a judge, I have sometimes seen partnerships in the dressage arena between young children and small ponies, or between adults and solid 'ordinary' cobs, which on that day outshone anything offered by expensive Warmbloods and professional riders – and which brought tears to my eyes because of the quality of the relationship that shone between them. I have often joked – but it isn't really a joke – that one of my own best dressage experiences was when I took our schoolmaster, Lolly, off down a local bridleway one autumn day to pick sloes for sloe gin. For perhaps an hour he manoeuvred just as I asked, very precisely back, forwards, sideways, at this angle and that, to allow me to reach the branches I wanted, standing patiently and still while I was actually picking from the saddle. He then walked calmly home with the heavy plastic bags that contained the sloes balanced across his withers. His attentiveness, calmness and accuracy in responding to my aids and positioning truly demonstrated the level of his skill and the best quality of our rapport. We had thoroughly enjoyed ourselves together.

It is interesting, in the light of this ideal of a rich and attentive communication between horse and rider, to consider again the three collective marks which are given to the horse at the end of the dressage test sheet.

Paces *(freedom and regularity)*

Impulsion *(desire to move forward, elasticity of the steps, suppleness of the back and engagement of the quarters)*

Submission *(attention and confidence, harmony, lightness and ease of the movements, acceptance of the bridle and lightness of the forehand).*

Clearly, training plays a large part in the horse's ability to develop a correct way of going, to perform the movements and to make fluent transitions between them so that the test becomes a whole rather than a series of add-on bits and pieces. But much of what is required depends upon the quality of the rider-horse relationship. Freedom in the gaits is to an extent genetically determined – but a rider who is tense will block that freedom or impair the rhythm. Many a free walk on a long rein is better demonstrated on exit after the final halt than across the long diagonal in the middle of a test! A horse's willingness to go forward is more a matter of enthusiasm and confidence than one of response to a nagging leg. Elasticity, suppleness and engagement in the horse demand from the rider a soft, following seat, a generous hand and appropriate opportunities for rebalancing. And without such a partner, the horse cannot, even if he wishes, offer the confidence, lightness, acceptance and ease which are together labelled as 'submission'.

In a way, we could truly say that the collective remarks, though ostensibly about the horse, actually tell us more about the rider. And when we receive our

Freedom and regularity; impulsion; elasticity; attention and confidence. Nikki and Lolly at Hickstead.

test sheets, it is helpful to bear this in mind, because we can always change ourselves whereas we can only hope to change others through the way we behave towards them. We can develop our sense of rhythm; we can learn to think 'forward' instead of unconsciously holding our horses back because it feels safer; we can learn to stabilise and at the same time elasticise our contact so that we show our acceptance of the bridle; we can work at developing skill in the following seat, and its necessary companion, the active seat, so that we become truly supple in the back; we can behave in a way that elicits trust and attentiveness. We cannot expect the horse to do any of these things on his own without actively matching him item by item.

■ Read the collective mark descriptions again carefully, and give yourself an honest mark for each.

■ Then give yourself a separate mark for each item listed under each heading. Which items do you need to work on, and how might you go about it? Do you need more information (reading, videos, your trainer)? Do you need help in assessing how you are doing (a trainer or experienced friend)? If you have been competing, look at your test sheets – but apply the comments to yourself in order to gain additional information. What if it said *you* 'fell to the left in halt', *you* 'were not in front of the leg', *you* 'lost rhythm in the lengthening' etc? Looking at it this way may be an uncomfortable process – but it is one you can work on. And remember, too, that any praise and good marks belong to you in exactly the same way! 'You made an excellent transition', 'lovely rhythm', 'very straight', 'calm and flowing', 'really promising' – those are yours too.

In this, as in everything else we do with our horses, it is helpful to remember that what happens is feedback, not failure – or even success, for if we don't know what we did to achieve the success we cannot repeat it. *How* did we get that lovely rhythm? *How* did we get that soft downward, or balanced upward, transition? *How* did we achieve what one judge called that 'essence of straightness'?

Working with Representational Systems

■ Take a moment to look back at the notes you made when reading Chapter One (or to remind yourself, if you didn't make written notes) about the representational system(s) you naturally prefer.

■ What are the advantages to you of this kind of processing?

■ Which were your less-favoured systems? What disadvantages are there in being less cued in to these senses?

■ Do you know anyone who is naturally comfortable and fluent in using these senses? Can you talk to them about what it is like for them, and how they do it?

Both here and in the title of this chapter I have deliberately found common phrases which say more or less the same thing while using language drawn from one particular sense. You can do this too. For example, *I'm tired* might be expressed as *I'm worn out* (K), *can't see straight* (V), or *feel faint/fading away* (A – or possibly also V).

- Take each of the following phrases and find ways of expressing the same idea using other representational systems: *They don't see eye to eye. We ran into some problems. They seemed so in tune.*

- How would you translate into sensory language the description *'He/I/they didn't understand'*?

- Build up the habit of listening to the language other people use, and working out what system(s) they use most often.
  Write down (or, better still, speak onto tape) a brief description of an everyday experience. Then listen to it carefully and note your own language preferences.

- Then, think through the experience again, asking yourself what else you might notice. For example, if your description was mostly visual, ask yourself what you would be feeling (physically), and what you might be hearing. (This is called sensory overlapping.) Would there be any smells? or tastes? Take time to build up a richer replay of the experience. You may still naturally feel the visual way of representing your experience is 'more you' – but you now have the possibility of other options, and more choices.

You can do this with any number of scenarios – pleasant memories, imagined scenes of relaxation, dreams of the future, and you can apply it to your riding, too.

- Take a specific movement which you understand and which you think you and your horse do well – or at least adequately! Begin with something which is relatively straightforward and quite well-defined. For example, a canter departure on the correct leg; a halt; a trot-walk transition; a small circle; trotting freely forward over poles.

- Replay it in your mind. If it helps, write down a description.
  Now note which of your senses was most involved.

- If you were *seeing* the movement, were you seeing it as if from inside your own eyes, or as if watching from outside. Was the image in colour? Was it sharp; bright; close to or far away? Moving or still? Were your eyes focused or defocused? Were you looking ahead, or down at the horse's neck? If you were watching yourself, what was your vantage point – from high up; from above; from the side; from the middle of the arena as if lungeing?

▪ If you were *feeling* the movement, were you aware of rhythm; pressure; temperature; balance? How aware were you of different parts of your body – what your seatbones felt; your shoulders; your inside leg; your outside leg; your hands?

▪ If you were *hearing*, what were you hearing? The horse's footfalls? Were they loud; soft; crisp; thudding; close; distant? Did you hear your own breathing; the horse snorting; sounds around the school?

It is quite likely that these questions may suggest additional possibilities from within your own most favoured sense. Many people haven't thought about whether they see things from inside or from an outside viewpoint until they are asked, even if they know they do see them. Many people know that they feel things physically, but not that they can get in touch with the experiences of different parts of their own body.

As we saw earlier, this outsider viewpoint is called **dissociated**, whereas the view from inside is an **associated** one. Both have their uses: the associated view is usually more 'in' the experience and therefore more immediate and vivid (it may have more links to feeling, too), whereas the dissociated view gives you some distance – literally – or a different perspective.

▪ Take a riding event: find out how you naturally see it, then practise seeing it the other way. What difference does this make? Now, you have a choice – you can do either, or both, according to what is most useful.

As you reconstructed your internal experience of a particular situation, you may well have found that more than one sense was involved. In this case, it can be useful, as well as interesting, to notice the order in which you did what. NLP calls this **sequencing**, and we often develop personal patterns of sequencing, particularly where feelings are involved. For example, one rider might imagine riding a test (**visual, associated**), then at the end switch and see herself from the outside, spectator or judge's view (**visual, dissociated**) as she comes to the final halt. Depending on the way she looks at things (literally), this might lead to a good feeling (**kinesthetic**) – or a bad one. There might also be some **internal**

dialogue going on, for example: '*I should get placed for that*', or: '*She won't think much of it because judges always see him as small, fat and hairy, however soft and obedient he is.*'

These thoughts and feelings can be noted down as a sequence running like this:

visual (associated) ▶ *visual (dissociated)* ▶ *kinesthetic* ▶ *internal dialogue*
V(a) ▶ V(d) ▶ K ▶ ID.

(Internal dialogue can be really powerful in its effects, and is explored more fully in Section Four and in some of the Case-studies.)

Sequences can be really important because, as we know, 'one thing leads to another'. You might realise, for example, that for you personally, seeing yourself (dissociated) often leads to some critical internal dialogue. If you change the sequence, you can change the 'reality' of your experience.

Another person might run a quite different sequence, beginning with a kinesthetic processing of the test, then checking out how they look from an outsider view (visual dissociated), making corrections to their kinesthetic processing according to what that view showed them, and ending with a view from inside their own position (visual associated) as they run the movement better. So their version of the sequence, in NLP notation, would run:

Kinesthetic ▶ *Visual (dissociated)* ▶ *Kinesthetic* ▶ *V(associated)*
(K ▶ Vd ▶ K ▶ Va).

There is no 'right' or 'wrong' way of processing: but there can be more effective ways than those we are used to, and ones which give us new options.

Later on in the book I shall look again at sequencing, since it can play an important part in issues of confidence: how we sequence our internal processing (our thinking) can reinforce our lack of confidence, or can be an essential cornerstone of success. But we can take charge of it, rather than simply continuing to experience it because 'that's how it's always been'.

When I asked you to identify not only which sensory system you tended to use but also its details – for example, whether visual images were coloured or black and white, whether bright or dim, close or distant, I was asking about another important feature of our thinking, one which NLP calls **sub-modalities**. (The representational systems are 'modalities' of processing: finer details such as hard, soft, weight, lightness, etc are therefore 'sub'-modalities.)

It can be really helpful to become aware of which sub-modalities are most important for you: these are the ones which make good experiences as good as they are, and bad ones as awful. A rider I know tended to replay her old trainer's comments in her head as she rode: since he was very critical, she felt criticised and despondent, and so tended to ride worse. When we worked on this, she found two options helpful. One was to substitute a friend's helpful comments for her old trainer's. But even more effective was to change the tone of her trainer's voice, exaggerating it so that it became whining and miserable. This made him seem ridiculous, undermining the content of what he had said, so that she began to ignore him, and eventually forgot to give him an airing at all! In her case, it was the tone which mattered, rather than the words. Another rider, who was fearful of being run away with, ran clear, large, coloured scenarios of this in her head. Not surprisingly, the possibility seemed pretty vivid – and therefore more likely. It helped somewhat if she made the images smaller; but what really made the difference was to fade the colour and to stylise the image so that her horse looked like one in an old hunting print, with his legs all stuck out in unrealistic prancing poses and a snooty fox watching from under a hedge. This amused her, and so made the idea more ridiculous. And once something is ridiculous, it tends to lose its power.

■ Take a riding situation which you really enjoy. Find out how you represent it to yourself, and in particular which sub-modalities are most important for you. Try changing a number of sub-modalities in turn to discover what differences this makes – and put them back again if changing them spoils or diminishes the experience for you in any way. But keep any changes that help!

■ Now take an experience you enjoy less, and alter the sub-modalities you have found to be significant for you so as to improve them. (How does lungeing on a wet day seem if you brighten the colours, or turn up the sound of the birds?)

■ Next, take an experience which you find unpleasant or which makes you fearful, and find out which sub-modalities are the key to the unpleasant or fearful feelings. Experiment with changing them until you find a way that makes the experience better. Often, bad experiences are coded in bright colours, loud sounds, strong feelings. What happens if you dissociate and go outside the experience, or tell a story about it instead of being there? What happens if you put soft, soothing music with it? Bad experiences may be seen as close-to, or moving rather than static. What happens if you freeze-frame/pause? Or make the images static, or black-and-white?

One of the strange and marvellous things we learn in all this is that we do not have to continue being the victims of our own thinking. We can learn how to change it. And this is not telling ourselves a lie: a frightening or dangerous experience we had was indeed that – but we don't need to replay it over and over 'in glorious technicolour', or project a repeat of it over any anticipation of a similar event in the future. That was then – but we can keep whatever we learnt from it while lessening its power to frighten, depress or disempower us in the future.

Let's look at how some riders used representational systems and submodalities to improve their riding.

One rider I worked with was a very good visualiser. She visualised, in fact, as she was riding, seeing what she wanted to do almost as if it were a film projected in front of her. It's very likely that she was riding with her eyes defocused, since this happens automatically when we 'go off inside' our heads. As she rode, she was seeing herself doing what she was actually just about to do – for example, a small circle in the corner. But she was so busy seeing that happening out there ahead of her that she wasn't preparing for real here and now. So when she actually got to the corner she and her horse weren't prepared and balanced to do the small circle after all. The picture in her mind – a moving image – had been so real that it got in the way of the performance she wanted.

For her, it was helpful first of all to recognise that this was what she was doing. Then, she experimented with ways of bringing her attention back to the here-and-now, finding that how and where she focused her eyes was very important. If she continued to stare off into space, she stayed 'inside her head', going into a kind of trance. As she trained herself to flick backwards and forwards between what she was actually doing now and her image of what she wanted, she was able to use the future image as a guide, and to check how her real actions were contributing to it. The future image could then become like a compass to guide her, rather than a mirage to distract her.

Another rider had a strong visual awareness, which had helped him from the very beginning of his riding to know what correct positioning was, and to model his own performance on that. As a result, he quickly achieved an enviably upright upper body posture with a good lowered heel and correctly bent elbow. However, because he was much less aware of the kinesthetic dimension of his experience, his efforts to maintain correct posture tended to make him rather stiff, and in trying to keep his heels down he was at first unaware that he was bracing the knee and lower leg. Once he learnt to get in touch with how his body was feeling, he could appreciate what was going on. Interestingly, he found it worked best if he then added more information to his visual representation of his riding: he learnt to see the difference between a stiff and a flexible back, and to check this in himself by dissociating for a moment or two to gain an observer's view. He also learnt to 'watch out for' the flexibility he needed in the knee and ankle. The image of coiled springs in these joints, yielding and returning, helped him too. It was not necessary for him to 'give up' his visualising, only to become aware of how it could limit him, and to find ways of modifying and enriching his internal experience so that it worked for him better.

Riding is a communication that requires us to be sensitive and skilled kinesthetically: yet, as I've shown, all our senses can play a part in helping (or hindering) both externally and internally. And I want to add in here a further pattern which NLP has identified, and show how it made the difference that makes a difference for one rider – my own trainer, Debby.

NLP grew from observing and from noticing patterns. There is one pattern which most people are unaware of: when we process internally through our different representational systems, our eyes move in ways which are not random, but which are reliably connected to the particular representational system we are using. NLP has been able to map this out.

When we are remembering something visually (Visual remembered, Vr) we tend to look up and to the left.

When we are picturing something in the future (Visual constructed, Vc), we tend to look up and to the right.

When we are replaying something we have heard (Auditory recalled, Ar) we look horizontally left.

When we imagine something we will or might hear (Auditory constructed, Ac) we look horizontally right.

When we are involved in Internal Dialogue (ID) we look down left.

And when we get in touch with bodily or emotional feelings (Kinesthetic) we look down right.

If you want to use any of these systems deliberately, it helps to look in the appropriate direction. And you will notice in conversation how other people's eyes move in these ways quite unconsciously as they think or speak.

This connection between internal processing and eye movements is, of course, one reason why many riders look down. They are getting in touch with how it feels, or how they would like it to feel. This poses a problem, because, however slightly, it weakens the seat. Clearly, not all riders look down, and few look down all the time. That's because there is yet another way our eyes can reflect internal processing: they just widen and go out of focus. You can see this happening in conversation when people stare off past you into space for a moment or two. In a good light you will see that their pupils are dilating.

Kinesthetic focusing: Debby and Alsace at Hickstead.

Defocusing: Debby and Merlin. Merlin is showing temper, as his tail and open mouth indicate. Debby's calm expression and defocused eyes are both outward signs of her inner concentration, which enables her to maintain her effectiveness when being challenged.

*Nikki and Vals.
Nikki is tuning in
kinesthetically and
Vals is dropping
onto his shoulder.*

*Riding defocused:
Nikki and Merlin.
In contrast to the
previous picture,
Nikki is giving Merlin
security through
her more connected
seat and legs, and his
calm concentration
reflects this.*

*Debby defocusing –
with 007.*

*Debby and 007:
kinesthetic focusing.
Although 007 is round
and stepping well
under, he is less
'uphill' than in the
previous picture,
which was taken in
the same working-in
session.*

Leo and Lolly: kinesthetic focus. Looking down has rounded Leo's back and lifted his heels.
Lacking the security of his rider's seat, Lolly is lifting his neck and coming off the contact.

If we want to access internal processing when we're actually riding, the way that really works best is to defocus. In her book *Ride with Your Mind*, Mary Wanless called this 'soft focus', because when we defocus we don't stop seeing things – they just go blurry as we 'look through' them.

Photos of Charles de Kunffy or Arthur Kottas riding always show them upright and looking off into space: my guess is that they are defocusing.

My trainer, Debby, trains with de Kunffy and Kottas herself and is a successful competitor, teacher and judge. Her one major limitation as a rider was that she looked down. This compromised her seat, good though it was, and in competition it made her less visible to the judges, as though her body was saying 'I'm not here'. She knew about this and corrected her posture when she remembered – but she kept forgetting and looking down again because she is strongly kinesthetic.

Talking about this one day, I suddenly thought of suggesting that she might defocus instead. A couple of days later I went to the yard. Debby was already riding in the school – and what a difference! Upright, taller, deeper seated, more confident-looking – and feeling. The next day she took her own horse out to a competition, winning one class and coming second by just one mark in another. On the same day she and Vals really attracted the eye, and were placed. Debby said that she noticed she was even more able to feel what was happening with the horse than she had been before: their communication had got even better. You can see the differences clearly in the photographs.

Defocusing. Karen and Billy, proud and purposeful and in touch with each other.

- Where do you look when you are riding? What is happening inside? What difference does defocusing make for you?

- Watch riders you admire. Where are they looking?

In personalising your learning from this chapter, and applying it to yourself and your riding, the first concern is always, what do you want? When you know your goal, then you can use these and other skills to help you achieve it. In doing so, you can also enjoy playing with the 'reality' of your internal experience, and discovering how much play can, in fact, create what becomes real.

CHAPTER 7

Lopsidedness

We are built differently in each of our sides. We are certainly right- or left-handed, depending on functions of our central nervous systems. As a result of one side predominating, our musculoskeletal progress also develops unevenly… Yet, the goal of most athletic endeavours is to attain trained (learnt) ambidexterity. We certainly propose ambidexterity as one of our major gymnastic goals for our horses. 'Straighten your horse and ride him forward'.

CHARLES DE KUNFFY *Training Strategies for Dressage Riders*

The ingredient of good posture is the one that … allows you to be direct, swift, efficient and harmoniously satisfactory to yourself.

MOSHE FELDENKRAIS *The Master Moves*

Why does our horse need to be ambidextrous? Surely that matters only if he is going to be a top-class performer? I have chosen to devote a whole chapter to the question of lopsidedness because, rather than being an 'optional extra' just for dressage horses it is essential for the health and well-being of all ridden horses. And in endeavouring to make our communication with them as effortless, flexible and effective as we can, we need to become ambidextrous too.

The Horse

The essential, and often forgotten, reason why a horse needs to be ambidextrous is that it will help him live longer, more comfortably and with less strain. And this is the essential underpinning of all flatwork schooling. De Kunffy reminds us that when we take the horse out of his natural environment and ask him to carry a foreign weight on his back – the unsupported 'bridge' between the four pillars provided by his legs and the weakest part of his anatomical structure – we owe it to him to help him develop a fit and elastic musculature which will support the shocks and burdens of the rider's weight as well as carrying his own with less effort. Additionally, we need to train him in a way of going that protects his joints from unnecessary shock and strain and to train ourselves to ride with the least possible bouncing and jarring.

That is the physiological aim of a 'correct way of going': it is a way of moving which is fit, easy, smooth, elastic, balanced. In addition, we have to teach the horse to adjust his posture and movement so as to bring his centre of gravity, which is naturally nearer his forehand, closer to his rider's position and his own centre of motion, which is further back. The closer his centre of gravity to where the rider sits, the better the horse's balance in carrying this foreign weight. Therefore he has to learn to step further under himself and to lower his quarters by tucking his pelvis under. This also helps him develop his back muscles, adding to his fitness and ease, even if he is never asked for advanced dressage movements such as piaffe.

The Rider

Classical training, therefore, aims at economy, effectiveness and ease of movement, in both horse and rider. And in order to achieve it, we need good communication skills. Being one-sided is a great gap in those skills. It is rather like trying to speak a foreign language without knowing half the tenses. Certainly, we can get by with a present tense, a bit of future and one workable past tense; but we can't have a proper conversation, or understand much more than simple questions and answers.

In our everyday non-equestrian lives we can get along well enough with one-sided dominance: we describe ourselves cheerfully as right- or left-handed, as though that were unchangeable. There are, perhaps, a few times when right-handers find that an inconvenience: for example, trying to paint in a corner with the 'wrong' hand; or when the dominant hand is injured. Left-handers also come up against daily irritations and handicaps: the way tables are laid; smearing what they write as they write it; implements (such as scissors) which are designed for right-handers; pen-sets in banks and building societies, which are invariably placed to be convenient for right-handers…

Such inconveniences also affect our communication with our equine partners. And, as usual, we tend to frame our awareness of it as being largely to do with the horse: 'He won't go off the left leg' could often be translated as: *My left leg is weaker than my right;* 'He goes quarters-in on the left rein' as: *I tend to turn slightly to the right;* 'He falls out when we are turning left' as: *I collapse my left hip and throw away my right contact when we are turning left.*

The issue is not one of blame. It's not his fault if he is one-sided – indeed, many people argue that horses have a natural 'handedness' just as people do. It's not our fault if we are one-sided, either. Riding, more than other things we may be involved in, just happens to be something which requires us to address that.

He offers what the rider is asking for...

Version A – crooked down centre line: rider pulling on left rein, collapsing hip, horse's quarters to left.

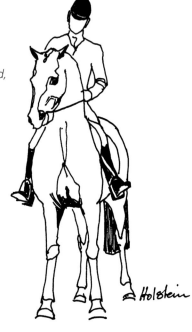

Version B – crooked halt: rider unbalanced, turning horse slightly to right.

Rider collapsing left hip, losing outside contact: horse falls out through shoulder.

How can we go about this, and how can NLP help?

First, as the earlier chapters of the book have shown, NLP provides us with many ways to refine our ability to observe and assess what is going on, and to measure that against how we want or need things to be, and then, later, to evaluate how effective we have been in changing the situation. Calibration and contrastive analysis are both valuable tools here, as is our awareness of representational systems and an ability to use them flexibly. The principles of the ROSE also help us to build better ways of communicating and clearer, more achievable, outcomes. NLP frees us to concentrate on how things are, how they could be, and what works – using a whole range of mind-body approaches.

On 28th December 1999 the *Times* carried an article about the poet Ted Hughes' daughter, Frieda Hughes, who is a painter. I was interested particularly in a little, almost throwaway, paragraph:

> Her first portrait… got Frieda short-listed for the prestigious Moran Prize in Australia. Moreover, she injured her right arm in the middle of painting it and was so frantic to finish that "I sort of flipped my brain over and carried on with the left". "Then," adds Laszlo [her husband], "When the arm got better she painted with both hands."
>
> What? with both at once? "Yes, I still do that sometimes". And it is a good picture, vital and assured.

Knowing that handedness is controlled by the opposite hemisphere of the brain was part of the secret. But how she 'flipped her brain over' is not described – and for her, it didn't need to be. If you know anyone who can use both hands, one option is to ask them how they do that. But actually, we all do many things with both sides of our bodies – or we could if we put our minds to it (and again, that everyday phrase tells us what is required). We may all be unconsciously limiting our ambidexterity – simply by not attempting to exercise it. The case-study of Karen shows some ways in which the rider's ambidexterity can be developed on and off the horse.

Improving Ambidexterity

So, if we want to improve our horse's ambidexterity and/or our own, we first need to know where we are starting from. Then we need to work out what we might do (or ask him to do) to improve. Then we need to assess again, and to evaluate the difference. Is it enough? If not, how can it be improved further? And so on… Because of its nature, riding is never 'finished'. Every moment of every ride is part of a cycle of assessment, evaluation, attempts to improve, followed by assessment again… We are always evaluating the present state as against the desired state we have in our minds, and our actions are ongoing attempts to move closer to our desired aim or goal.

I would like to offer you a variation of this model, using a key word **ADEPT** as an acronym to help you remember the processes. It gives us a series of specific steps we can take towards the meaning of the word itself. Adept, says the Oxford Dictionary, means *one who is skilled in all the secrets of anything.*

A ssess

D iagnose

E xercises

P ractise

T est

And of course, each testing leads to another assessment… and so on… Like riding, the process is never finished.

Becoming adept

Assess The place to begin is by knowing where we are beginning! For most of
D us, as Mary Wanless points out in *Ride with your Mind*, lopsidedness is
E so familiar a state that we don't notice it – and in fact feel far less
P comfortable when someone helps us to position ourselves correctly. So
T sensory acuity will help you know when you are doing something
different, because initially it will feel odd! However, we need to know first what to correct.

You can train your observation by focusing on ambidexterity when you are watching other riders competing. Take one or two, and concentrate just on straightness and the extent of the ambidexterity which rider and horse display. Test movements which happen on both reins (and most do) allow you to use contrastive analysis – but you will need to find your own way to hold the first example in memory until you can compare it with the second. Practise memorising what you see (V) and what you hear (A). How is the picture different on the second rein? Is the rhythm, regularity or the definition of the footfalls different the second time?

So far as your own riding is concerned, this is the place for an observer on foot and/or a video camera. Sometimes as a judge I notice lopsidedness, in either horse or rider, and I will try to comment on both. For example: 'Less flexible to the left', 'quarters in on this rein', 'rider sitting to left', 'rider sitting against the

Rider collapsing to the right – 'marbles in the right ear' – horse overbending in neck. Wendy and Vals.

movement' (turned to the outside of a circle rather than into it). But the best time for a comment really is while it is happening, so that the rider can feel it and attempt to correct it there and then. Watching on video allows the rider to see what is going on, but the adjustment then has to be made later. Both are valuable aids. Your trainer, if you have one, is likely to be commenting on this already. If you don't, perhaps you could arrange with a friend to swap observation sessions with each other.

■ Make a list of the differences you find. Probably, this will come to you naturally in a negative form of words – for example, 'doesn't bend so well to the right'. Now put this into the positive form of a goal, remembering that the first rule of a well-formed outcome is that it should be stated positively. What *do* you want? *I want my horse to bend equally flexibly to left and right. And in order to achieve this, I want him to bend more flexibly to the right than he does at present.* Continue making your list, translating each item into a positive form. Now you have a list of your specific outcomes in relation to symmetry.

A
Diagnose
E
P
T

Next, you and your helper or trainer need to work out where the lack of symmetry is coming from. Is it the horse, or you? Is the problem one of physical limitation (for example, one hock weaker than the other), or of genetic predisposition (most horses bend more easily one way than the other), or is it in the mind? In this case, it might be what NLP calls a 'learnt limitation' – as, for example, when a horse who has been injured in the past learns to avoid putting stress on the injured side, and continues to do so even when the injury is healed. This can apply to riders, too, as shown in the example I gave earlier in the book of my 'remembering' to protect my long-ago broken ankle.

Is it perhaps just a problem of habit? You've always done it this way and never thought about it? Our own posture on turns may be a good example of this: I am sure that people don't turn their bodies in exactly the same way to both sides – but if you turn your hips, shoulders and weight slightly differently on a horse it gives him a different signal, and his way of turning then exaggerates the difference!

One of my own asymmetries is to sit more heavily on my right seatbone – maybe caused initially by avoiding weighting my injured left ankle. Some years ago, I used to exercise six horses on one day once a week, and noticed that I was losing a strip of skin under my knicker elastic on the right side. I blamed one of the saddles: I was sure its seam came just in that place. How could the owner put up with it? Only more recently, when the same began to occur on my own well-padded saddle, when I knew more about asymmetry, and when my trainer was commenting on how I slid out to the left, did I realise that the problem was how I was sitting! In this case my horse's own asymmetry compounded the problem: Vals has a weaker left hock and tends not to raise the left side of his back until really warmed up (or unless asked really emphatically). So the right side of his back is often more raised, I slide out towards the left, thus collapsing my right hip and sitting more heavily on my right seatbone... For so long as I remain lopsided in this way, I make it harder for him to correct his asymmetry: for so long as he remains lopsided in this way, he makes it harder for me to correct mine. But I am the smart partner, so it is my job to initiate changes!

A
D
Exercises
P
T

As you diagnose possible causes, you can begin to work out what will help you and your horse correct the imbalances or lack of symmetry. Some exercises can be used to help the horse alone – for example, you might use lunge work on small circles to build strength in a weaker hock without the additional burden of your weight. Some can be done together – shoulder-in can help the horse use his inside hind more fully and build its flexibility and strength. It is important, however, that you exercise him equally on both reins even if you are trying to strengthen one – otherwise you will be producing another kind of asymmetry!

After all, if his off hind finds it easier to bear weight, it won't find it a problem, and the same amount of exercise will help the near hind. And you won't be accidentally developing other imbalances or asymmetries by doing more work one way than the other.

■ Work out a programme of exercises with your trainer or a knowledge-able friend, and estimate how long it may be before you will be able to establish a real difference.

Some exercises are for you. Get your observer to help you make a list of what you need to address, and when you are riding pick just one thing to think about each time, otherwise you will be overwhelmed with 'musts', 'oughts' and 'shoulds'! But remember that you can also work on symmetry without your horse. You spend far more time off him than on, and so you have plenty of opportunities in everyday life to make yourself more ambidextrous.

■ Use your hands as ambidextrously as you can for ordinary everyday tasks. You can even practise writing with your non-dominant hand: it's amazing how it can begin to learn to manage. The development of fine finger and wrist skills will erode the 'dead hand' syndrome which riders often suffer from – and it may even come in useful for writing if your writing hand is ever injured. Be inventive! Think about swapping your shoulder bag to your other shoulder, carry your shopping (or the bucket) in your other hand, mount and dismount from the offside for a change…

A
D
E   Then it is time to practise. Incorporate your symmetry-building
exercises into your everyday life and your schooling routines. You
don't need to make a big issue of it, to the exclusion of other things
Practise you are working on, or you and your horse will get bored. But just
T   ensure that each time you are together you do something that helps.
If you are in the stable, you can work on symmetry by making sure that you do things from both sides and with both hands. Saddle him from the offside as well as from the left. Use both hands when grooming. Put his rug on from either side, not just one. And when you are at home or at work, remember to try some everyday tasks with the less familiar hand. It can actually be quite fun. And practice is a sure way to get the message into the muscles – yours and his.

A
D
E
P
Test
As you progress through this sequence, you are testing each time how much closer you have got to your desired state. It's like walking with a map and a compass: your desired state is where you are heading, your diagnosis is your map and your exercises are the compass that guides you in the right direction. Practice is each and every step you take along the way. Where a step takes you off-line, where you feel you aren't making progress, for example, you can take the information as feedback and experiment with something else. Don't keep on with something that doesn't seem to be working – be flexible! Otherwise you will just be taking another step that takes you further off-line.

Although the model seems to come to an end, any Test of the situation is really the beginning of an Assessment again. In riding, there is always something more that we can do. But make sure that you do have a clear, achievable desired state for each session – for example, to do a couple of really good, flexible, soft circles on each rein. Then you will have a clearly specified goal (an essential element of a well-formed outcome), and you will be able to determine how far you have achieved it – or what you need to do next to make it even better. You might think that a couple of good circles isn't much result for a whole session – but if you are really able to say that they were better than before, and that you and your horse achieved more symmetry in doing them, then you can be very pleased. Finish your schooling for the day on that good note: if you haven't used up all your allotted time, do something simpler and fun, so that you are rewarding yourself and the horse and making sure that he gets the message that he has done what you wanted.

In this chapter I have looked at the perennial problem of how we work towards overcoming the built-in asymmetries in ourselves and our horses. And in exploring this, I have used a model which can also be used in many other life situations. The ADEPT model, which I have designed specially for this book, is a way of measuring our progress towards what we want to achieve.

The more skilled the rider, as we all know, the less he or she seems to be doing. Developing our ambidexterity means that our communication can become both elegant and economical: the greatest secrets of the skill are those of achieving more with less.

CHAPTER 8

Who's Leading Whom? Breaking Limiting and Negative Circuits

A horse can only understand corrective guidance that shows
him what to do, not the kind that shows only what not to do.
CHARLES DE KUNFFY *The Ethics and Passions of Dressage*

The tradition of aiding is based on the philosophy that horses will
perform when helped rather than compelled, that only a happy
frame of mind will result in a relaxed frame for the body, and
that compulsion soils the mind and spoils the body with tensions.
CHARLES DE KUNFFY *The Ethics and Passions of Dressage*

Systems resist change because the parts are connected. However,
when they do change, it can be sudden and dramatic. There will be
particular places where you can effect large changes with very little
effort once you understand the system. This is known as leverage.
JOSEPH O'CONNOR AND IAN MCDERMOTT *The Art of Systems Thinking*

In this chapter I am going to look at how NLP can help us understand and
change the 'stuck patterns' that we often get into with our horses. I called the
chapter 'Who's Leading Whom' because it's often difficult to tell: where did
the problem begin? It's like family arguments – sometimes some trivial incident
or other starts off a whole scenario or even a familiar dialogue, perhaps involving several people. The argument didn't really start with that incident – that was
only a trigger for an existing pattern. Similarly with our horses: one moment
things may be going fine, and then all of a sudden we're into a tussle we've had
many times before. That old pattern is recurring: he's doing what he usually
does, we are responding as we usually do, and here we go again. Maybe it will 'all

end in tears', or maybe it will remain a low-grade disappointment; maybe we'll get cross with each other; maybe you or I will chalk it up as yet another failure to 'sort it out', yet another obstacle to what we really want to achieve. A fair amount of energy, both mental and physical, will be wasted.

What can we do to change this? NLP offers us ways to understand what is going on, new perspectives from which to view ourselves and our equine partner as we repeat this mutually adjusted manoeuvring, and – most important – some really powerful leverage for change.

Stuck Patterns in the System

What kinds of patterns might be involved? Here are some possibilities you may recognise:

- Horse belting off when asked for canter and then running through the bridle despite the rider's determined attempts to regain control.

- Ignoring the leg aid by falling out, or in, or not going forward, poor steering, hanging on the fence.

- Lack of attentiveness.

- Bad manners in the stable.

- Anxieties about 'normal' events such as shoeing, clipping, loading, hacking. Spooking at everyday objects. Resistance to being caught, or groomed, or having the bridle put on.

While I have described these in terms of the horse's behaviour, all of these problems also involve a human partner, and I have argued earlier that it would be possible to define the same problems in terms of the rider's contribution. For example:

- *Giving an abrupt canter aid; allowing the horse to become unbalanced onto the forehand; attempting to slow the horse with the rein not the seat.*

- *Over-busy legs; 'boring' or 'nagging' the horse with the leg or spur;*

- *Failing to get the horse in front of the leg; looking down not where rider is going; too lax a frame offered with the rein; legs weak or rider relying on the rein to steer.*

- *Rider too passive; schooling too repetitive – horse has become bored; not enough variety in horse's life; rider 'dawdling along' without clear goals.*

- *Rider doesn't set clear boundaries; boundaries are inconsistent; horse is allowed to do his own thing when it doesn't seriously inconvenience the rider; rider afraid to challenge poor behaviour.*

- *Horse not prepared for the activity; rider attempts to lead without first pacing; haste or other concerns or preoccupations mean that rider is less 'there for' the horse; previous bad experiences have left residual anxiety and horse has not been sufficiently reassured.*

- *Rider has not taken time to break the feared activity down into smaller and more manageable steps (chunking down); rider has not set up 'rehearsals' so that horse can become used to the process without pressure.*

Another set of issues which more clearly originate from the rider are those which relate to assumptions and beliefs: for example, '*He can't do medium because he's not built like a Warmblood*'; '*I'm never any good on Friday nights, after a long week, so I think I'll just give him a bit of a spin to exercise him*'; '*He's too old to learn now*'.

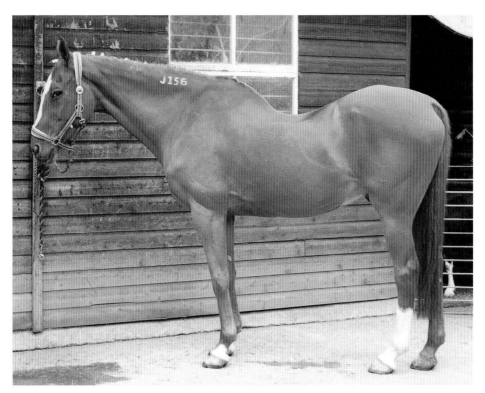

Lolly in his skin – 'not built like a Warmblood'.

Though these are the rider's beliefs, they will be communicated to the horse by the rider's behaviour, so they then set off forms of behaviour in him which, in turn, elicit further behaviour in the rider.

The rider and horse partnership can be seen as a **system**, because they interact with each other and affect each other in a variety of ways – physical, emotional and mental. But as I've shown earlier, each is also a system in his or her own right: a system made up of interconnecting body-mind processes. And the basic implication of a systems way of thinking is that if you change one part of the system in any way, there will be effects on other parts of the system. If you change how the rider thinks, you also change the rider's feelings and physical behaviour. If you change the physical behaviour, you change the rider's thinking and actions. And so on. If the rider changes, the horse changes in response. Similarly, if anything changes within the horse system, it affects other parts of the system. When a horse is unwell, or tired, he may become depressed or irritable. As he gets older, he may become grumpy. If we ask something difficult of him he may become anxious – and half a ton of anxiety is pretty anxiety-inducing for us! If he becomes so absorbed in his own perception of the world through his excitement or fear, he will ignore our puny input into our shared system – and that can be annoying, terrifying or potentially dangerous.

The rider-horse system. Rider drives, horse hollows. Or does the horse hollow and the rider then drive? Wendy and Vals.

Calibrated Loops

Where patterns between partners become repetitive, NLP calls them **calibrated loops**. They are loops because they go round, and calibrated because each party in the relationship (rider and horse, in this case) reacts in turn to the other partner, leading to a dialogue.

Looping may be productive or unproductive in its outcomes. A schooling session or test which begins with a clear 'statement of intent' by the rider, paces the horse well as he responds, and continues with sensitive leading that relates to what he offers, is likely have good results. If this becomes a repeating pattern, it is also a calibrated loop – though one which will not give the rider cause for concern! However, it is as useful to spend time seeking to understand a productive, effective or pleasant calibrated loop as it is to study a dispiriting one. Only when you know how such a beneficial loop is constructed have you got the means of reproducing it.

In order to show how calibrated loops work and how we can shape them differently, I'm going to take an everyday example from my own experience, and outline a seven-step model that can help us get unstuck and move on. First, here are the steps.

---

1. Model the loop

2. Brainstorm possible changes. Remind yourself: what you allow, you teach. What you repeat, you reinforce.

3. Remind yourself of your positive goal.

4. Remember whose job it is to move things on!

5. Identify what you can change.

6. Ask yourself: 'What stops the change I want? On what logical level is the block?'

7. Check: 'What would happen if I did make the change?' Deal with any negative consequences you anticipate.

My Problem

Our younger horse, Vals, is a strange mixture of attentiveness and lack of attention, stubbornness and wishing to please. When he is working at home, especially, he is distracted by virtually anything going on around him, though he can also concentrate completely (for example in competition or when part of a display). He is affectionate and likes to please and be praised – but he will also offer less than he is capable of, and show passive resistance on occasion. He can be a joy to ride – or hard work!

Step One: model the loop

Work out in as much detail as you can what the elements of the loop are. You may find it helpful to write it down in a step-by-step dialogue. As you do so, include your own representational system processing, including internal dialogue, as well as what actually happens. How you feel, and how your horse seems to feel, as the dialogue progresses are important parts of the sequence, which not only result from what has gone before but which also influence what comes next.

Vals takes a while to get into the right mood to work. At the beginning of a schooling session he will loosen up quite willingly, but he doesn't offer to go forward very much. This tends to involve offering a shorter stride than he can, bending his hind legs minimally and not powering forward. This means that for some time he is not really in front of the leg. My contribution to the loop is to allow this. In my work as a therapist I'm really good at pacing my clients. I tend to work at their pace, using the opportunities they offer to gain insight or make changes. Even though I am effective I'm not often pushy or confrontational. This pattern of behaviour can be a strength – but in my riding it's a weakness, because it allows the horse to set the pace and take charge.

Vals not in front of the leg: Wendy allowing.

I also have some beliefs that feed into this: as will be clear from this book, I believe that, on balance, horses are good-natured and that resistances are learnt. So far so good: but I now think this overspills into a further belief which may often hamper my effectiveness in riding. This is a belief that horses will naturally want to cooperate with their riders, and that if I only approach mine in the right way he will want to go forward 'of his own accord'. This belief is really based on a wish, not on hard evidence. If I follow my own NLP teaching – why would a horse wish to go forward unless I have shown him that it is in his own best interests?

So, if I don't make my expectations clear each time I ride, my horse will offer what my actions tell him – in this case, my passive acceptance will communicate that whatever he offers is okay. I then have to struggle to retrieve the situation, because I actually want more than this – I just didn't make it clear to him in the first place. This in turn tends to feed into my own self-doubts about my ability as a rider: maybe I'm not really all that good… More often than not, we will spend fifteen or twenty minutes at his pace, and only the rest – the last twenty minutes or so – doing something useful.

I need to pace him for a shorter amount of time – but also to pace in a way that keeps his attention and makes the point that this pacing for this length of time at the beginning of schooling is deliberate (a period of stretching and warming up) rather than letting him set the tone. So I could ask him to walk with purpose rather than just dawdling along, require him to do some work moving off the leg even though he is on a long rein, ride large turns and circles so as to keep him attentive, and so on.

▪ Take a stuck pattern you have with your horse. Model it in detail. Write down the sequence of the interaction between you.

Asking him to walk with purpose. Wendy and Vals.

Step Two: brainstorm possible changes

Remind yourself of the NLP presupposition that *If you continue to do what you've always done, you'll continue to get what you've always got*. Where the pattern is a stuck one, you need to change it, because each time it repeats it becomes ingrained further.

> If I don't make my intent clear from the outset it allows Vals to set the pattern – but he doesn't have an intent or outcome for the session as I do, so in effect I could be allowing our activity to be directionless. It's like taking a taxi to catch a train, then telling the driver: *'Oh, just go where you fancy'*. Every time I allow the pattern to repeat, I'm reinforcing it.

■ What are you allowing – and reinforcing? Remind yourself – you can change it!

Step Three: remind yourself of your positive goal

To change the pattern, you need first to be clear about what your goal is, and to find a positive way of framing it. As the quotation from de Kunffy at the beginning of this chapter reminds us, horses can only be corrected by being shown what *is* wanted: negative guidance, if we think honestly about it, is really just punishment. It stops where it is: it doesn't lead on.

> What do I actually want in schooling Vals? I want him to be attentive, forward and between hand and leg, and I want this to happen from the very beginning of a schooling session. In fact, I want it to be a habit – even if he is walking on a loose rein to stretch his back muscles. It's the attitude I want as well as the behaviour. We both need to be paying attention!

■ What do you really want in your situation? Write it down – positively!

Step Four: remember whose job it is to move things on

As ever, it is the rider's responsibility, wherever the problem is coming from. De Kunffy reminds us that the rider is the 'smart partner on the back of the strong partner'. We are the ones who can look at the situation differently, to generate different approaches, to change the pattern of the calibrated loop. If we do something different, take something out or add something in the horse must respond differently. That is the essence of calibration. And the one thing we can be really sure of, is that he is a brilliant instinctive calibrator of what he sees, hears, feels, smells and tastes. Insofar as he is also a creature with a long memory, and a liking for habit, he can build up a body of meanings for the things that regularly happen to him: that is the basis of training. And if we change the input we give him, and build it into a new pattern, we begin to create a new calibrated loop.

On one occasion, Vals and I were schooling, and the pattern had begun to run in its usual way, aided no doubt by the fact that the school was wet and we had to avoid several boggy patches. I was losing enthusiasm. So was he. Our work was half-hearted, but though I recognised this I had not reached the point of frustration plus determination where I usually begin to turn things around. When Vals is not truly between hand and leg he tends to drift towards the fence – and he had a perfect excuse (or even a reason) on this occasion because of the need to avoid a boggy patch. I was jerked out of my rather dismal trance state by a heavy blow to my knee: we were so close to the fence that I had run into a plank that had come slightly adrift and was sticking out. It could have caused a very nasty injury, though fortunately I was only badly bruised.

At this point I wanted to give up: pain and a feeling of incompetence both overwhelmed me – together with a feeling of hopelessness and some internal dialogue about 'I can't do this; it always happens; I'll never change it; it's all too much hard work'. For a few moments I thought I would give up on the session and go in. And if I had, the pattern would have gone on… and on…

■ What kind of leverage would help you feel in charge of your situation again? Might it be a reframing of your role, as it turned out to be in my case? Or a memory of a previous success you've had in problem-solving…?

Step Five: identify what you can change

This brings us to the crunch: what to change and how to change it. *The Art of Systems Thinking* offers us some useful 'Generative Learning Questions', and to illustrate how useful they can be as prompts, I've worked through them myself in relation to my problem with Vals.

- **What are my assumptions about this [issue]?** *As I've begun to explore, my assumptions about the nature of the horse can be helpful because they lead to a positive attitude towards him, but because I generalise them further to cover his attitude to his work,* **I start to depart from the actual evidence** *and in fact to set myself up for problems. My belief has acted as a distorting filter.*

- **How else could I think about this?** *I need to think more systemically and more assertively.*

- **What else could this [set of events] mean?** *He is bored and in fact feels I've lost interest in him because I'm no longer paying him attention. He may even be feeling less secure. He's not getting enough feedback. He's testing me because I'm less clear in telling him what I want than Debby. He's asking – do I really mean it?*

- **How else could this be used?** *I could see any difficulties as an opportunity, or reminder, that I need to take charge of myself and turn the session around.*

These questions all invite us to step outside the immediate situation and view it (approach it, get hold of it, hear it) differently. Each provides us with more information. Sometimes this is enough in itself. If we get stuck, it tells us that we don't have enough information, enough resources or enough skills. We need more, if we are to move on. Being stuck is feedback; the questions are one way to get more detailed feedback which we can use to make the changes we want.

> ▪ Use the generative learning questions to work out in more detail what you need to change.

Step Six: ask yourself *'what stops the change I want?'*

Often, this question directs your attention to the point of greatest leverage in the system. If you find out what stops a change, you also find out where the change needs making. It can also be helpful to refer back to the Logical Levels model to find out on what level the desired change is being blocked.

This is another example of what NLP calls an ecology check. It gets us to assess the effect of one thing on the system as a whole, whether the system is that of the rider, the horse or the interaction they have together. This gives us a way to ensure that what we are planning doesn't lead to undesirable consequences, or interfere with something else which is actually useful to us.

There were two things that stopped me making the changes I wanted. One was my belief about how my relationship with Vals ought to be. The other was the state I was in. What acted as a lever for me was a reframe: my husband Leo was schooling at the same time, and when I said I was giving up he reminded me that Vals hadn't worked long enough: he needed more exercise. This reframed my role into one of trainer with a responsibility for my horse's welfare as well as his training – and with the reframe went a change of state. *You're right*, I thought. From a despairing and inadequate rider, I was transformed in an instant into a competent and determined trainer. For the next twenty minutes I ignored the pain in my knee, and asked very clearly for the kind of work I wanted. Off the fence, off the leg, forward, attentive, on the bit, through the back. And that was what I got. The leverage needed to be on that part of the system that was stopping my desired change: my own beliefs and state. Once these were shifted, the behaviour shifted. I do have enough of the skills I need to ride my horse effectively – but I don't believe it strongly enough or for long enough. When that is added to my professional habit of following, we end up with a calibrated loop that is dispiriting, ineffective for training and ensures that rider and horse both under-perform.

What stopped the change I wanted was a complex set of behaviours resulting from my beliefs. Reframing the state which went along with the beliefs changed the behaviours and resolved the situation. I didn't have to change the beliefs at that point because I could simply switch to a parallel set which go along with a different role I have: that of trainer. But I am now aware that if I continue to maintain my idealistic vision of how the horse might be expected to effectively train himself without my asking him, I shall run into the same problems yet again. We will go round the loop yet again. I need to separate my belief about the nature of the horse, which is enabling on the whole, from my beliefs about training him. I need to recognise that being clear to him about what I want is in fact *more* consistent with my beliefs. Having no clear purpose and direction is actually less kind and less supportive to him than showing him clearly what I want. How else is he to know if he is valued?

What stops the change can be many other things: it might be a lack of skill (capability); it might be a question of environment. And, as the next chapter explores further, past experiences in the rider have often led to learnt fears or limitations. Once we have identified the blocking point, which is usually also the point of most leverage, we can work out what kind of lever we need to use.

Believing differently, asking differently. Wendy and Vals.

Change may also be stopped by what we imagine its consequences are likely to be. Sometimes succeeding can let you in for increased pressures – from yourself, your trainer or your friends and family. It can seem better to under-perform – unless you recognise and can deal with those half-imagined results.

■ What stops the change you want? What would be the consequences of making the change? Are any of them negative? If so, what will you need to do to prevent those consequences and still be able to make your change? Where is your point of leverage?

Step Seven: assessing the consequences of change

This optional step entails asking yourself a related question which helps you to check this possibility: 'What would happen if I did make the change?' Be aware that while the answers that first come to you may all sound positive, you need to listen out for hidden doubts, fears and anticipations. 'Well, then I'd have to…', 'Well, that might mean that…'

■ And if you did…? Are there any hidden issues you need to take care of before making your change?

In this chapter I've looked into the problematic question of stuck patterns, and how NLP and particularly Systems Theory can offer us both some understanding of what is going on and some ways to become unstuck. Stuck patterns use up lots of energy in a way which is unproductive. It's like the record going round and round in the same groove. While there is movement of a kind, it is going nowhere: no progress, no growth, no development. The energy invested in the repeating pattern may be accidentally dispersed – or sometimes it may 'blow a fuse'. We need to break the circuit and then redirect the energy onwards. The steps I have outlined give you a way of doing this; and you can draw on ideas and strategies from other parts of this book to help you.

In summary, I'd like to repeat a set of questions from *The Art of Systems Thinking* which usefully bring together the kinds of questions we can ask ourselves when we recognise we and our horse are in a calibrated loop:

- What is the relationship… ?

- What am I doing that could be triggering his response?

- What is he doing that is triggering my response?

- How does my response trigger his response?

- What relationship do I want with him?

- What response do I really want from him?

- If what I am doing at the moment is not working, what, if anything, stops me from doing something different?

Adapted from O'CONNOR AND McDERMOTT The Art of Systems Thinking

Once we recognise the pattern, step outside our own position and begin to ask these questions and work with the answers we get, the energy that was bound up in the stuck situation can be freed, and help take us and our equine partners forward again.

CHAPTER 9

Competition – Getting in a State

No serious riders ever believed the training goal was to compete.
They believed that you rode a horse to unfold his natural potential
until it was fulfilled and the horse could offer no more physically
because he had no more genetically defined talents to display.
CHARLES DE KUNFFY *Ethics and Passions of Dressage*

There are no unresourceful people, only unresourceful states.
JOSEPH O'CONNOR AND IAN MCDERMOTT *Principles of NLP*

Early in this book I described what states are. For example, when de Kunffy teaches, his state involves all the logical levels. He demonstrates a calm stillness of body and his voice has a low tone and minimal inflection, so that it is less disturbing for the horse and focuses the rider on the content rather than the manner of what he is saying (behaviour and environment). He feels what the rider is likely to be feeling, and understands (capability) how to help them correct and improve performance through his observational and communication skills. He believes that each pupil deserves the same full attention, whether first or last in the day, and that during that time their needs come before his needs. This state is summed up, for him, as one of self-effacement (identity) and attentiveness to the needs of his pupil: he reminds himself of the army saying '*Shut up and serve*'. All of these together constitute his 'teaching state'.

In the previous chapter, I used the example of Vals and myself to illustrate a calibrated loop: showing that what acted as the circuit-breaker and freed our energies was a change of state. Leo's reminder that Vals had not worked enough acted as what NLP calls an *anchor* (in this case, an auditory one) for a more resourceful state – one where I felt and behaved as an adequately skilful trainer rather than an ineffective rider. The work that I did after the event meant that the next time I rode I was able to replicate the training state and be resourceful and effective from the beginning of the session. But because I am used to a pacing state I may have to remind myself for a while of the need to switch into my more active training state in riding before it becomes fully automatic.

In this chapter, I am going to explore how the NLP concepts of *states* and *anchoring* can help us with the often problematic issue of competition, allowing us to understand and work more effectively with any problems we and our horses have when we go out into the world and let others see what we can do.

States

As I've explained, states occur as a normal, natural, ongoing part of life. They are set up, maintained and activated through experience and through modelling others who are influential for us, and they can easily become habitual. They can involve some, or all, of the logical levels: identity, beliefs and values, capabilities, behaviours and environment. And because the unconscious part of the mind stores information through links and associations, two other things also follow: states can be triggered without conscious awareness by any element in a complex situation; and they are not immediately changeable through conscious intent.

Let's take an example. Karen was anxious about hacking. Specifically, she was alarmed by the orange container lorries which operated from a depot near her home. At a conscious level, she worried that her horse might be frightened by them and shy or bolt – but actually she was more bothered than he was, communicating her fear to him so that he too became generally tense when hacking. Since she wanted to be able to hack without anxiety, she asked for my help. We explored the problem from a number of angles, and at some point I asked her what aspect of the lorries most alarmed her. She immediately replied that it was the colour; and this seemed sufficiently unusual to explore further. Expanding on this, she said that she hated orange, and – now she came to think of it – had nothing that colour in her home or her clothing. I asked her if she knew why orange had unpleasant associations for her. She said at once – surprising herself – that her parents' kitchen had been painted bright orange, and there had been many rows there when she was a child. Once we had worked on these earlier memories, she was able to break the link with the colour, which had been a chance one anyway; and after this the container lorries were no longer a problem. Once she had stopped reacting to them, so did her horse.

This example shows us how a quite unrelated part of a bad experience – the colour of the room – had for this rider become a visual anchor to tension and anxiety. When she saw anything that colour, it automatically triggered similar feelings. No doubt the fact that the lorries were large added to the issue – but the fact that her horse lost his tension as soon as she lost hers showed that her state of anxiety was the root of their problems. The half-forgotten and certainly unconnected memories triggered mind-body changes, rapidly producing a state which then itself became linked with hacking.

This example is an unusual one which illustrates the process well. But we have all had many experiences of being judged; and depending on what happened and how we felt, we too can be triggered into old states when we go out to ride before others in a competition.

■ Spend a few minutes jotting down your experiences of being judged: at school, in tests and examinations, answering or performing in front of others. What kind of mind-body states did these experiences trigger in you? Do they in any way resemble how you feel when you compete nowadays?

■ Are these states resourceful ones for you, or unresourceful? In what ways?

■ Which logical levels are most involved?

■ What kind of representational systems are most active when you are in your competition state?

■ What kinds of things trigger your state?

Experiences of being judged. Wendy and Lolly.

Anchors

An anchor is any stimulus that becomes linked with a particular state and can then subsequently trigger the same state, and so it can work through any of our senses. It may be logically connected to the state or quite accidentally associated with it. As a family, for example, we tend to be alarmed by early-morning telephone calls, because some years ago we had a call at breakfast time that told us our young horse was dying of colic. It only took that one call for us to learn an automatic feeling of dread each time we get an early-morning call. The mind is very good at one-shot learning!

On a happier note, many anchors can be associated with, and lead to, good feelings. Many showjumpers, for example, can be seen wearing faded and rather tatty hats – hats which for them became 'lucky' because they were wearing them when they won a particular event. And even though they are very unlikely to have won every event in which they have worn that hat since, the very act of putting it on can make them feel confident. Logic plays no part in 'good' anchoring any more than in 'bad'!

 ■ What kind of state does competition produce for you? How is it anchored?

NLP identified and named the process of anchoring; but in doing this it has also helped us recognise first that anchors can be changed and second, that anchors can be created deliberately. We don't have to be stuck with outdated, or limiting, anchors from our past; and we can also learn how to anchor states that we want to be able to access at will.

Competition

What are the sorts of things that may happen when a rider is competing in an unresourceful state? I have listed some common possibilities, and left some blanks for you to add any others of your own.

- Dissociating – seeing oneself (usually critically) from the outside.

- Judging oneself harshly.

- Running self-critical or depressing internal dialogue.

- Imagining disaster scenarios.

- Focusing on own worries and feelings and losing attentiveness to the horse.

- Becoming anxious or fearful or tense.

- Communicating tension to the horse.

- Losing concentration.

- 'Going blank'.

- Forgetting the test.

And when we are in an unresourceful state, it will, of course, be communicated to our horse. When we were discussing this, de Kunffy said to me:

> Horses never know they are in an Olympics… The rider conveys a crisis, so the horse will act tense because he will participate in the rider's crisis… The horse wears his mind on his body. His emotions are instantly displayed in bodily tensions…

So our very anxiety itself can bring about the difficulties we may have been fearing.

Breaking the Pattern

Considering the goals

How do we get out of the negative cycle once it has begun? It can be useful first of all to ask ourselves what we are competing **for: what is our goal?** My reason for choosing the particular de Kunffy quote at the beginning of this chapter is that it reminds me that the goals that humans have for competition are theirs, not the horse's – and, further, that we ourselves can have a range of possible goals, each of which will have different implications for the state in which we compete.

De Kunffy reminds us of the classical rider's goal in training: to develop the horse to the utmost of its genetic potential. In working towards such a goal, what part might competition play? Perhaps to offer the rider a benchmark of how far the horse has progressed in his personal development programme. Perhaps to offer the rider/trainer some helpful suggestions for what they could do to aid this programme. With this in mind, a judge's comments can help to reinforce the rider's role as trainer rather than be taken as implying a judgement on their degree of adequacy as a person. In other words, they could be understood as comments on capability and behaviour, not on identity. And it is always easier and less threatening to receive feedback that is pitched at the lower, rather than the higher, logical levels.

If the rider believes that the value of a test is as an assessment of the horse's standard of training, what kind of state is this likely to create? For some riders, it will be enabling. For others, though, it may be experienced as a reflection on their skill, or lack of it, leading to an uncomfortable, unconfident state. As de Kunffy said to me, '*Competition may be one of the greatest spoilers of the rider's mind.*'

What happens if we ask ourselves what a test means *to the horse* – and therefore, what it should mean to us as his trainer and friend? In our conversation, de Kunffy said: '*Riders should ride the horse, not the test. A test is for a judge, but they should ride it for the horse's sake, for the benefit of the horse. We are riding to cheer up the horse.*'

This is one of his arresting and thought-provoking ideas: it makes us wonder. How can our riding 'cheer up' our horse? If we have such a goal in mind – especially when we are riding a test – it will certainly make some important differences to how we feel and how we approach the test! It reminds us that riding both can and should be a means of creating pleasure – for both partners. The expression 'cheer up' implies that the horse could actually feel better for being ridden. How we can bring about such a desirable state by the way we ride is a great question for us to keep in mind, whatever we are doing and wherever we are doing it. And I suspect it wouldn't leave much room for anxiety about third parties such as judges!

Our riding, de Kunffy continued,

'…should always be without ego and for the good of the horse – very mindful of the horse's universe and how he feels about it. And then entering that universe and working from an insider's point of view outwards… The horse should not even know it's a competition. The horse should just think he's working with pleasure because he's balanced and he's supple and relaxed and his mind is focused on the rider and he's trusting. These are the pleasures of the horse, and these pleasures reconfirm themselves and generate new pleasures.'

I believe that if we could genuinely feel that this was our goal in riding, not only at home but in competition, it would focus our attention back on the horse and on reaffirming a pleasant and harmonious partnership with him even in the arena. The judge would become largely a spectator, fortunate enough to be watching. And this state of harmony and mutual concentration would be achievable whatever the level of the horse's training. A soft, obedient, confident Preliminary or Novice horse can be as much a joy to ride or to watch as an Advanced one. The joy of watching a fluent, expressive horse working at a high level is not dependent on the difficulty of the movements: if performed well, their beauty only adds to the pleasure of the rider and onlooker, because it has been produced as a result of the high quality of horse and rider communication.

So for some, perhaps many, riders, a different goal in training and competing could produce a very different and more resourceful competition state. But not everyone will find this easy, partly because it involves beliefs that we are not very familiar with. How many of us were fortunate enough to have teachers who made it clear to us that what we learnt was *our* possession, that what we achieved was important because it added to *our* enjoyment of life? That exams were a benchmark of *their* effectiveness as trainers, as much as of *our* ability as learners? Some of these views were expressed by educationists in the nineteen-sixties and seventies, but even then they were thought of as 'radical'. To think of learning as being the possession and achievement of the learner, and the role of the trainer as assistant in that process, constitutes a major reframe of long-established views and would be contrary to the personal experience of many people.

▪ What are your beliefs about the place of competition in your horse's training – and your riding life? Would you like to change them in any way?

If we see the goal of our horse's training as being the full development of his potential, we accept that our job is to help him discover how to do what his physiology, and his character, will allow him to. Some horses enjoy going out to competition just as some people enjoy parties. Others don't. Some are outgoing and expressive; others are sensitive and apprehensive. If we attempt to ride from the inside out, we will be using the understanding of our unique, individual partner to pace, reassure and lead him sensitively in this situation as much as we aim to do when we are at home. I have sometimes heard judges comment that a rider who effectively interrupts the test being ridden to deal with the tension or bad behaviour of the horse even where it means departing from the set movements 'is only schooling him now'. Often, the rider concerned is a professional, more readily cued into training mode by encountering problems. So far as the judge's comment is concerned, it often seems to imply that the rider has in some way given up on the proper purpose of the test. Certainly, if you decide that a horse who refuses to halt properly needs to be asked again, you will forfeit marks, and you will be schooling. But if we remind ourselves that the horse learns from every communication, whether intended as such or not, what will he be learning from being allowed to jiggle about and throw his head in the air, or back away from the bridle? Neither pleasure nor good learning comes from this. If you need to be firm with him or reassure him in the halt, or you use a firm half-halt on another occasion to rebalance him when he tries to run through the bridle, it will probably lose you marks – but the overall movement will be improved, and you will be teaching him something useful rather than allowing and therefore reinforcing an unwanted behaviour.

What will he be learning?

Dealing with personal baggage

So far, I have been concentrating largely on the experience of the horse, and exploring how the rider's goals can affect him in competition. But what about the rider's own experiences of competing or being judged – which may come from quite different contexts in life, perhaps preceding any association with horses? If we are aware that we bring our own past baggage with us every time we compete, and that this can get in the way of competition being pleasurable, we have the option of working on ourselves.

Probably, as you answered the questions I asked earlier in the chapter, you will have been reminded of a range of feelings and events that have come together to make your own personal baggage about tests and being judged.

- If your experience has been good, ask yourself how that has helped you when competing. If it was good, but somehow it hasn't transferred into riding situations, ask yourself what are the differences between the two situations: use contrastive analysis to identify where you could make changes.

If your past experiences of being judged have left you with a negative legacy, a first step in dealing with this is to remind yourself that that was then, not now. You survived the experience. If you think about that you then, what would have helped? Perhaps there was information that you didn't have; perhaps you didn't realise that you had many other qualities and skills worth having, even then; perhaps you didn't know you would overcome that problem; perhaps you didn't realise that the person judging you was really unfair – or, on the other hand, only accidentally so. In thinking through past events with the extra experience of adulthood, we can often 'feed in' valuable corrections which in turn change the way we hold the memory. It can be rather like editing a film or audio tape, or adding a voice-over which, through its commentary, makes a very different meaning of the experience.

It can be useful to remind yourself that the person judging you today is not the same person whose judgement upset or undermined or frightened you in the past. Almost certainly, your judge is or has been a rider too – and is therefore only too familiar with the kinds of situations and problems you might be encountering. For the same reason, the judge will be really pleased to see you doing well, and will be, like de Kunffy, in some sense 'riding with you'. If the judge is sensitive, the comments will reflect this empathy. Such judges remind

Preparing to be judged: Wendy on Lolly and Nikki on Fred working in, with all the weight of their 'baggage' upon them.

themselves each time they judge that competitors always want to do their best; that they feel proud and protective of their horses and want them to do their best too. Therefore, they will try to give you helpful rather than critical feedback. And if that is not the case – and we all have moments as judges when we don't manage to live up to our ideals – you can remind yourself that you did the best you could on the day.

 ■ How might you helpfully edit some of your old experiences of being judged?

Anchoring resourceful states and feelings

You wouldn't go into a test without preparing yourself and your horse, and without practising the test. In the same way, you can help yourself a great deal by preparing the right frame of mind. Here is a step-by-step process for bringing this about: it's the process of positive anchoring.

● Think of a time when you and your horse were really working well together. Replay it in your head, several times, making sure that you involve as many representational systems as possible. Your favourite, or **lead**, system will probably come first and with most detail: continue to add by asking yourself what each of your other senses can tell you about that situation, until you have the fullest representation you can make.

● Think of at least one other good experience. If you have good competition experiences, use them, but it's more important to pick times when the communication and rapport between the two of you was at its best.

● You can also use non-equestrian experiences, since what you are after are feelings of confidence, calmness and competence. Any feelings that will help you in the arena, wherever you have originally experienced them, can help. (There will be more about this in Chapter Ten.)

● Take a moment to re-explore each experience, and to discover what detail most encapsulates its peak for you. Was it the moment when you felt your horse just sit under you into that calm and perfect halt? Was it the moment when you saw the softness in his neck? Was it the rapidity with which he 'just knew' you wanted him to canter almost before you actually asked, so that he was there, on the aid, ready? You are looking for the 'YES!' moment. This is what you want to anchor. And what kind of state did this bring about in you? One of confidence? One of skilfulness? A training state? A think-on-your-feet state? You may want to anchor more than one. Confidence is really useful in some situations: quick-thinking can be more useful in others. The more specific you can be, the more targeted and the more effective your anchoring.

● Find an anchor for each of your chosen resource experiences. Anchoring is about finding and then using a trigger that takes you into your resourceful state whenever you want, just by activating it. You want something that is easy, rapid, central to the meaning and effect of your experience. It's a key to it, a peg on which it is hung, a summary, a way in. It could be a word. It could be a picture. It could be a sensation or a sound. It might be a phrase: 'You can do it!' that you say to yourself. Anchors can also be kinesthetic – a small, unobtrusive movement such as a deep breath, or a slow eye-blink, are good examples. In riding, you will have to pick a movement which communicates consistently to your horse rather than giving him an added, perhaps irrelevant, message to your intentional aiding. So your kinesthetic anchor will need to be a movement you can do in any gait and any dressage figure.

- Think again of the experience, and as you reconnect with it and get back the essence of its meaning for you, call up its anchor. Zoom in on the picture, feel that momentary feeling, say the phrase to yourself, make the slight movement.

- Now do something different, perhaps something quite mundane. Try washing up, for example; or skipping out. Or even just think about doing them. NLP calls this **breaking state**, and the reason for doing it now is to give yourself the chance to test and build the effectiveness of your anchor. You got the positive state you wanted: now you need to banish it and know that you can get it back again – all in a flash. In the middle of this actual or imagined mundane activity, call up your anchor, and notice how it brightens up even a dull set of events. (You can also break a negative state if you change your activity, body posture or the focus of your thoughts.)

- Practise using your anchor to call up your resource states at all sorts of times in all sorts of places. The more you use an anchor, the more reliable and more effective it becomes. What you are actually doing, as you practise, is to create new neural pathways in your brain. As you make the connections, your brain cells literally connect with each other by growing more of the filaments (dendrites) along which electrical messages pass. And as you repeat the process, you strengthen the links and make them more automatic. You are creating new helpful structures in your own brain.

- Once you know that your anchor works for you, use it in competitions or other situations where you want to experience those feelings it calls up. Perhaps you want to set yourself up by anchoring beforehand. But even in the competition itself it only takes a millisecond to re-anchor, or to use another anchor that is more appropriate to what is going on.

So far, I've been talking about anchoring our own resourceful experiences. But we can also draw upon the resourcefulness of others, by modelling them and anchoring that. When we model someone else, we make an internal representation of them: what we have modelled is now part of our own repertoire. We can find key moments that relate to them in the same way as we draw upon our own experience. Maybe the calm, erect stance with which they rode that perfectly straight, rhythmical, forward centre line is something that we can hold in our minds and use as an anchor. Maybe it's the calm, slow way they stroked their spooky youngster on the neck to reassure him before riding forward again. Maybe you can really feel the balanced lift of that fabulous canter departure they made. You can use models such as these to extend your resources beyond your own personal experience. You can also draw upon videos and photographs.

Perhaps your model is someone you know, and you can ask them more about what their own experience is like. You have a lot of information now about how people construct the reality of their experience, so you can ask the kind of questions that will tell you exactly how they do it. Then you can draw on their experience too. They may have beliefs about competition which make it less terrifying, or more everyday. They may have ways of concentrating and of blocking out distractions which lead to more fluent tests. They may have cracked a particular skill you have been struggling with.

Competition isn't such an awesome experience after all, if we think of it differently. To do this, we need first to become aware of how we currently think of it, and in what ways and on which of the logical levels this causes us problems.

Nikki and Lolly at Hickstead. 'He's balanced and he's supple and he's relaxed and his mind is focused on the rider and he's trusting. These are the pleasures of the horse.' (Charles de Kunffy).

If our current competition state is unresourceful, NLP offers us many ways in which we can alter and improve it. And if it is already resourceful, there are probably still ways in which we can make it even better – once we know how. And as we become more resourceful, so we free our horses of one of the burdens we impose on them, so that they too become freer to offer the very best they can on the day.

> If it is well done, a dressage test does not appear laced together from different movements but rather one continuous statement consistent in philosophy, feeling and existence.
>
> CHARLES DE KUNFFY *Training Strategies for Dressage Riders*

Getting it All Together

Should any part of the rider become stiff, the horse will respond likewise. If any part of either horse or rider is stiff, it spreads to the whole system.

CHARLES DE KUNFFY *Training Strategies for Dressage Riders*

CHAPTER 10

Self-confidence: An Issue of Belief

Think of something that you believe you can do and contrast it
with something that limits you. Determine the difference. Then take
the limiting belief and make it like the thing you can do. If something
stops you from doing it, find out what stops you.
DILTS, HALBRON & SMITH *Beliefs: Pathways to Health and Well-Being*

It starts with a belief, then it depends on discipline to make
this belief become a reality. And when it's a reality we have a
package of skills… It cannot be any other way.
CHARLES DE KUNFFY, personal interview

Being confident in ourselves or our abilities tends to help us achieve: lacking confidence tends to limit what we can do. Whatever the skill or task involved, confidence is like a tap that allows our capacity through – or limits or blocks it. But there are 'how-tos' for confidence just as there are for everything else. With the help of NLP we can model the processes that create, reinforce and undermine confidence, and so put ourselves back in charge again. And the place to begin is with beliefs.

Confidence is, above all, a matter of belief, not a matter of fact. NLP has shown us that we tend to act upon our beliefs *as though they were facts*. Where these beliefs are enabling, the more we hold on to our delusion that they are facts, the more they help us! Where the beliefs are limiting, their pseudo-fact status reinforces them. Because our need to filter information drives us to make daily use of those three handy simplifiers: deletion, distortion and generalisation, we will tend to find evidence that confirms the beliefs we started with. A loop is set up, in which belief leads first to action then to sieving the feedback we get from the action so that the original belief is confirmed. This is how beliefs become self-fulfilling.

The trap-like nature of some beliefs is more easily spotted than others. '*I can't get my horse on the bit*' be confirmed every time you ride. As is often the case, the trap is welded with words. *I can't* sounds innocuous – but implies a lasting state of affairs like *I can't reach that shelf*. Adding the magic word **yet** – '*I can't get my horse on the bit* **yet**,' or the equally magic phrase **don't know how to** – '*I* **don't know how to** *get my horse on the bit*' – points up factors we may have deleted without realising it. One is the time factor (*yet*). How long might it take me to learn this skill? The other is capability: I may not *know how* to go about doing this. The apparently simple phrase 'on the bit', as we know, covers a complexity of simultaneous happenings: the obvious rounding and yielding of the neck, the softening of the jaw, the engagement of the haunches, the going forward from the rider's leg with an energetic stepping under, the lifting of the back, the making and sustaining of the 'bow before the saddle' and the 'bow behind'. There is a lot there to 'not know' – **yet**! There's a lot for you to not know how to ask, and a lot for him to not know how to deliver – **yet**.

Some statements are even more slippery. What about the apparently 'obvious' statement that begins '*I'll never be able to ride him as well as my trainer, or jump him like the Whittakers*'. It goes without saying, doesn't it? They are professionals, they have access to top-class horses... Yet every time we make that kind of statement, to others or ourselves, we are reinforcing a belief which is self-limiting. The statement fools us by appearing to be a truth. Yet the one thing we can be sure of is that if we believe we won't, we will never find out if we might have. The Gilbert and Sullivan opera *HMS Pinafore* made a useful joke out of this generalising word never:

Never?

What, **never**?

Well, hardly ever.

And that shows a crack in the fixity of the belief beginning to open up.

This chapter is about how our beliefs affect our confidence as riders, for good and for ill. In particular, it is about working with self-limiting beliefs, decisions and strategies which have arisen as a result of past learning, so that we can free ourselves up to discover more of our potential, and more enjoyment, as riders.

A Strategy for Change

Belief, behaviour, capability. That is the sequence de Kunffy highlighted when we were talking together. If you start from a belief and add behaviour which is consistent with that belief, then you will begin to build the capability you are looking for. That is the basis on which he works: if the rider honours the beliefs and values of classical riding, and learns to discipline their own riding to be consistent with them, this will increase the rider's capability and enable the horse to make the most of his.

The same process, of course, occurs with limiting beliefs. You start with a belief, behave according to the belief and limit your capability accordingly.

We can have beliefs about anything at any logical level. We can have beliefs about identity, about beliefs, about capability, about behaviour, about environment. Here are some examples of these different kinds of beliefs:

Identity: *I'm a nervous rider.*
I'm too nice to my horse…

Beliefs: *You have to go in believing you can win.*
She's really successful because she has such faith in her horse.

Capability: *I'm too tired to ride well on Friday nights.*
He's not a Warmblood so he finds lateral work difficult.

Behaviour: *I get very anxious before competitions.*
It's only his first test so I hope we'll manage to stay in the arena…

Environment: *Those banners are very distracting.*
He works better when there aren't too many other horses around.

- List some of the beliefs you have that affect your confidence. Make separate lists for riding and non-riding ones. Are the riding and non-riding ones broadly similar, or are you more confident in one area than the other?

- Now sort them according to logical level. Are there any clusterings? If so, what does that tell you?

Where do beliefs come from?

Beliefs are derived from experience – ours and that of others who influence us. They can result from a single significant experience, or from a kind of drip-feeding through similar experiences. They may be modelled from a parent, teacher or inspirational figure. Sometimes they are summed up in handy phrases or proverbs, sometimes there are no words. Sometimes it's as though, at the crux of a significant experience, we have reached some kind of decision, which may be conscious or unconscious, framed in words or feelings, but which then binds us afterwards.

■ Have another look at the beliefs you listed, and see how many of them you can 'place'.

Confidence is about faith – not about blind faith. It's about having beliefs about yourself which aren't going to be dashed if you fail: in other words, valuing yourself without specific conditions. It's no good pinning your self-worth on winning that Elementary class, or learning how to do a half-pass, or getting that job. Confidence rests on having a sense of your own value apart from that. That is about confidence at an identity level. And if we can feel all right about ourselves, we pin less on issues of capability or performance (behaviour).

This may be where it is worth taking a wider base for your self-evaluation. You may be quite confident in some non-riding areas. What are they? What is the basis of your confidence? How could you incorporate this sense of self into yourself when you are riding? It is possible that, in riding, your confidence is limited by issues of skill (doubts about your capability or behaviour), whereas in some other areas of your life you take your abilities for granted, or feel more comfortable about them.

■ Make another list, beginning with the words *I can*. Include anything you feel confident you can do, whether or not it relates to riding, whether or not it seems important. 'I can make a good omelette'; 'I can keep to time'; 'I can be relied on if I'm asked for help'; 'I can type fast'. What do these things tell you about you?

■ Next, pick one 'can do' and ask yourself *how* you do it? How *you* do it. This is not about listing the ingredients and method for the good omelette, but what happens that results in *you* making one (including what happens inside you). Maybe it is about following a recipe – or maybe it's about being inventive with bits and pieces. Both are fine, but they are quite different. A methodical person goes about things differently from an inventive person. In riding, as in life generally, there will be different outcomes from the *how* of how something is done. What is your version? If you know, you can value it, and make the most of its strengths, whilst avoiding its limitations.

■ Then, make a list of areas where you believe you are limited. Pick one, and look at the *how* of it.

■ Then, use contrastive analysis. How is the 'can do' different from the 'can't'?

■ Find the difference that makes the difference, changing that in the 'can't' to make it the same as the 'can'. What happens?

■ Now take a riding example or two.... Use the same process to transform some riding 'I can'ts' into 'I cans'.

Imprints

Where a belief arises from a particular experience, NLP calls it an **imprint**. This is not thought-out, it's often rapid, but it's a lasting impression made by the experience. The naturalist Konrad Lorenz coined the term 'imprinting' to describe the instinctive attachment and modelling that he observed between young geese and the first thing they saw when they hatched. What they saw first, whether it was another type of bird, a human, or even his wellington boots, was what they followed, just as surely as if they saw an adult goose.

> An imprint is a significant event from the past in which you formed a belief…or a cluster of beliefs…What is important to us…about past experiences is *not* the content of what happened, but the impression or belief that the person built from the experience.
>
> DILTS, HALBRON & SMITH *Beliefs: Pathways to Health and Well-Being*

Some of the beliefs that affect our confidence in riding, for better and worse, come from imprint experiences. Perhaps you were lucky to have good early experiences. The authorial blurb in Dick Francis' novels usually begins: '*Dick Francis learnt to ride before he could walk…*' Since he went on to become a top jockey, and to write books in which the love of horses and of race-riding always shines through, it seems likely that his early experiences were positive. If you began to ride as young as he did, you may not remember any specific imprint experiences from that time; but there may be other, later, ones which you do remember. Perhaps you were praised, or achieved something special. Perhaps you were lucky enough to have a good imprint experience in a non-horsy context which you were able to generalise to many things you do, including riding.

Imprint experiences can lead to learning of many kinds. Earlier in the book I described how my experiences of cantering on riding school ponies imprinted a fear of cantering itself because it was then out of my control. When I was able to change the way I had coded the experience, my fear disappeared. Here is another example.

When we started riding as a family, some years ago, my mother used to come down to the yard with us. She was then in her late seventies. She liked animals, but was fearful of horses because once, when she was a girl, she had been in a friend's dogcart when the pony bolted. She had also seen milk-horses on their rounds bolting when something frightened them. So although she liked to watch, and help around the yard, she preferred not to get too close. After some time, coming to the yard several times a week and getting used to the horses, she began to get more courage, and to separate out these horses from her fearful beliefs about horses in general. She was also able to realise where her fear had come from, and to realise that working horses in the nineteen-twenties were much more likely to be suddenly frightened by the beginnings of motor traffic than modern horses brought up to the sounds and sight of tractors, cars and lorries.

One day, I was about to have a lesson on a four-year-old Lippizaner stallion we had in the yard, and my mother was walking down to the school with us. Suddenly she said: 'Do you think I could lead him?' I remember thinking, 'Should I be letting a lady in her late seventies lead a young stallion?' She was fit for her age, but lacked skill and strength to match him if anything happened. Then I thought that it would be great for her to have a good experience with such a horse (probably about as large and strong as some of the horses she remembered), and that while there was a slight risk, there was also a strong probability that a good experience would turn her fears around. So I walked on his offside, quite casually, but in my mind 'just in case', while she led him. And nothing happened – except that she had a triumph which helped dissolve a lifetime's fears.

When we want to deal with an imprint experience, we need in some way to revisit it so that we can change the way we have it coded, by adding in resources that we didn't have then, but have now. My mother was able to do that because she vividly remembered her earlier experiences, and yet gave herself an experience so different that it interfered with the old memories in a really useful way. In the present, she probably felt that she had support. I was with her, and our trainer was not far away. She knew more about horses, and trusted them more, than she had done as a girl. She also knew this particular horse, who was calm and amenable even though he was young and a stallion. This was a natural, one might almost say accidental, way of changing the effects of the early imprint experiences. And yet, of course, it reminds us of how all the processes which NLP has identified and can teach us are ones which occur naturally, out there, in the 'real world'. But why wait for a happy accident?

Working with an imprint experience

If you have an imprint experience that has limited you in some way in your riding, here is a set of steps you can use to change it for the better. Read the explanations right through so that the process is clear to you before you use it on something you want to change.

1. Rerun the experience in your mind as though you were watching it on a video, or hearing it told as a story. Keep dissociated, so that you are not experiencing the feelings again but only observing the events to gain information.

2. Pause. Ask yourself what learning there is from this experience. This is a reframing question, and it helps us to draw something from it.

Rerun the experience in your mind. Keep dissociated.

Holstein

3. Ask yourself what resources would have helped you then. Maybe you needed to tell yourself something. Maybe you needed support or encouragement from someone else who was there. Maybe you just needed to know that it didn't have to be like that, and wouldn't be in the future. Take some time to find out what would have helped. Let yourself remember how differently you feel, or have felt, at times when you did have those extra resources, or that helpful knowledge.

Remember how different you feel at times when you have those extra resources and knowledge.

4. Now in your imagination go back to before the limiting imprint experience, and run it through as if you *had* had that knowledge, support or extra resources then. The events themselves mean what they mean to us because of the learning we make from them. In rerunning the experience with the addition of these extra resources, you are likely to find that the meanings – and your feelings – change quite markedly, just as mine did over the issue of cantering. You may notice that as a result you draw quite different conclusions. The 'you' person you are observing is likely to be feeling very different, too. Notice the ways in which 'you' feel better.

5. Then, quite slowly, think through your subsequent riding experiences, noticing how different they, too, would have been if you come to them having had this changed experience and these new resources.Doing this allows your new resourcefulness and your different state to influence the way you have coded later experiences too. Once we know something, we can't *unknow* it: therefore the new knowledge or way of experiencing things will, if we give ourselves space to do this, affect our coding of many other events in addition to the original imprint event itself.

Summary:

1. Rerun the experience dissociated.

2. Ask what the learning was.

3. Ask what would have helped that 'you' then.

4. Rerun the experience, adding in the new information or resources.

5. Take yourself forward through your experiences since, noticing the difference the new resources make as you continue to recode.

Robert Dilts explains how this recoding helps us:

> Go through the entire negative experience making sure everything works out in a positive way. The next time you encounter a similar situation to the negative experience, instead of going back and unconsciously associating to what you did the last time... you now have a decision point with new choices. You'll be responding in a new way.
>
> ROBERT DILTS *Beliefs: Pathways to Health and Well-Being.*

Changing the effects of modelling

You can use a version of the same process to help with the effects of limiting modelling. Perhaps your family believed that it was 'boastful' or 'arrogant' to take pride in your achievements, or to 'put yourself forward' in any way. Many people brought up with these beliefs find it difficult to take pleasure in their successes, or to believe that they have the necessary ability to achieve what they want. The effects of this on competition are obvious – but actually the restriction is even more insidious and its effects more widespread, because it can mean that someone may judge themselves harshly, try only things they are pretty sure of being able to do, and not take risks. Confidence is an essential ingredient in being prepared to 'have a go' – because it is confidence, especially at the level of identity, which allows us to cope with not succeeding, looking an idiot, being ignorant, experimenting.

If you think you have been limited in this sort of way, use the same kind of strategy that I have just outlined – but instead of resourcing yourself, resource the significant people whom you modelled. Of course you are working with

Resourcing

STEP 1

Child: 'Look what we won!'
Dad: 'Don't boast.'
Mum: 'Think of all the poor children who don't have ponies.'

STEP 2

Q: What's the learning?'
A: He had a hard life, didn't show his feelings. She didn't want me to be picked on at school.

STEP 3

What would have helped? Thinks: It's okay to be proud of her, dad. Let her enjoy it, mum. You're all lucky she can have this fun. You've given her something she'll always remember.

STEP 4

'Well done, girl!'

'I'm so proud of you.'

'I feel great.'

'I feel good because she feels good.'

your impressions of them, not with the people who were actually involved – but it is your impressions of them then which are limiting you now! Put yourself in their shoes (take second position), rerun their experience, find out how they thought and felt, and what would have enabled them to feel differently, and to be less restrictive in the messages they left you with. If more than one person is involved, resource each of them separately.

You are likely to find important differences in understanding and feeling taking place as you work with their 'shadow selves' in your mind. After you have resourced them, and know how differently they might have behaved towards you as a result of having those resources, then you can rerun some of the same situations again, this time focusing on yourself. As you do, and as you experience how different things would have been with the different modelling you have now installed, your own feelings and beliefs will change. You can then take that forward into your present and future, in ways which the next chapter explores more fully.

Let's sum up. Because beliefs are based on past experience, they have powerful effects in shaping our expectations about the future. We carry them with us as templates, which shape the way we structure our internal experience and how we filter feedback. They guide our thoughts, feelings and behaviour, and our selection and interpretation of evidence. If we have *limiting* beliefs, we will inevitably behave in ways which limit us. We will be narrowing down the range of possibilities open to us. If we have *enabling* beliefs, we will be putting ourselves in the best position to deal with our experience and to shape and achieve the outcomes we want.

CHAPTER 11

Creating Your Riding Future

Remember that a rider who pursues his goals by riding his goals
will never achieve them. But a rider who pursues various logical
and proper means leading to a desirable goal will progress.
CHARLES DE KUNFFY *Training Strategies for Dressage Riders*

Thus, between wishing and having there must be doing. Furthermore, doing
requires a plan – a plan which guides your activity along those paths which
will (or are likely to) lead you to having what you want. Accordingly, we
have identified five stages in the process of going from wishing to having:
Wishing ► Wanting ► Planning ► Doing ► Having.
LESLIE CAMERON BANDLER, DAVID GORDON, MICHAEL LEBEAU, *Know How*

I have called this section of the book *Getting it All Together* because ultimately
that is what we have to do. Our dreams and hopes and intentions, our
internal and external skills, come together to create experiences with our
horses. And the essence of this is the fluency of our conversations. De Kunffy
reminds us that this experience is unique:

…the intoxication of having been a part of an art both as its creator and as one
created by it, both as a participant in it and as an inducer of it. For in classical
riding, the unit of horse and rider is both maker and made, both subject and object
of the art.

CHARLES DE KUNFFY *Training Strategies for Dressage Riders*

However much we may wish for such a state to exist between ourselves and our horses, we need to know how to make it happen. In this final chapter I shall look at some ways in which NLP helps us to translate our wishing into reality – a reality which itself is ongoing. And the case-studies that follow show us how some ordinary riders have used NLP to help them do that.

A famous golfer was told after winning yet another tournament that he 'had good luck'. 'Yes,' he replied, 'I've been practising it.' NLP is about practice, and the *wishing to having* model gives us a strategy for co-ordinating all the different skills we have to make our dreams happen.

'The unit of horse and rider is both maker and made, both subject and object of the art.'

Wishing

'I wish my horse would stand still while I mount…' *'I wish I could just win that other Qualifier…'* *'I wish I knew why he won't…'* *'I wish I had a better seat.'* We all have many wishes for our riding. Wishing is essentially passive: like winning the lottery, it often seems outside our grasp. And the first thing we can do is check whether what we wish for has the potential for coming true.

The Logical Levels offer us a simple and effective way to do this.

Logical level check

Ask yourself the following questions.

Identity: is what you want 'really you'? This is an important, and often over-looked, question. You might wish to see yourself coming down the centre line in the National Finals, but be unwilling to put the time in, even if you and your horse have the skill.

Beliefs: does it fit with what you believe and value? If riding is your way of relaxing, maybe it doesn't make sense to affiliate your horse and fill your diary with competition fixtures.

Capability: do you have the capability – yet? Do you know how to acquire it? It can be very important to be realistic here – because this helps us avoid the disappointment of setting goals which are either not achievable or only achievable in the long term. Breaking down your long-term goal (chunking it down) into a series of achievable steps is one way to encourage yourself as you go about building your capability. Knowing how to acquire the capability involves assessing how you learn best – and whether you are prepared to commit yourself to the varied costs of that learning.

Behaviour: what do you need to do? Can you do it (now or in the future)? What is the first step you can take towards making your wish come true? Is it something you can do this week, or today? If not, when? If you don't know, how might you go about finding out?

Environment: do you know where, when, how you will do it? This is about beginning to make your dream more specific, more attractive, more magnetic to you.

Wanting

> Though many people have no real separation between wishing and wanting, people who are consistently capable of turning their dreams into reality do have a separation between the two.
>
> LESLIE CAMERON BANDLER, DAVID GORDON, MICHAEL LEBEAU *Know How*

I said earlier that wishing is passive. Transforming wishing into actively wanting is a stage that takes our dreams closer to happening. And again, we can use NLP to help us. Wishing is often rather broad or vague. Adding detail and beginning to ask 'how' questions helps us move on to wanting. It also allows us to 'try our dreams on for size' and see how they fit. One useful way to do this is to apply the criteria of well-formedness, which were set out in the section on Outcomes in Chapter Four. These are ways to check that what you want is actually achievable. Another approach is to brainstorm a variety of possible futures. Is there really only one goal for you and your horse, or only one way for you to go about achieving it? The more acceptable options you have, the more chances of success.

> For example, when we bought Vals the idea was that he should be a family horse, like the others we had had: a bit of dressage, a bit of jumping, perhaps a bit of cross-country since Leo is bold and likes to jump. Vals was the right breed for dressage, and his grandfather was a top Soviet showjumper. But when it came to it, he showed no talent for jumping and a great deal for dressage. So our plans had to change. Leo generously deferred his hopes for a real jumper, and got on with making the best of his work with Lolly; but if he had really set his heart on jumping, we would have needed to part with Vals and find another horse instead.

Planning

It should be a feature of any plan that you make that it include *branch points...*

> The purpose of branch points in your plan is to help insure that you can still continue toward your goal if part of your plan goes awry.
>
> LESLIE CAMERON BANDLER, DAVID GORDON, MICHAEL LEBEAU *Know How*

Branch points are a really useful way of helping us stay in control. A long time ago I was helping a friend prepare for a job interview. We thought of everything, planned for everything, rehearsed everything – except the presence of other candidates! And it nearly threw my friend, because in her mind being interviewed had been a matter for just her and the interview panel. That taught me to think of everything that *might* happen, not just everything that *would*.

We can think of branch points in planning a training strategy, in managing a single training session and also, of course, in preparing for competition.

> When Karen took her horse, Billy, to a competition, the plan was that her trainer would warm him up, and then Karen would ride the actual test. This fitted with their usual schooling pattern, in which Jenny rode Billy first to establish the kind of work they wanted and then helped Karen continue it as she rode him afterwards. However, as Karen watched the warm-up the unexpected happened: Billy was behaving like a perfect gent, but another competitor's horse started misbehaving in a way that was becoming dangerous. Karen became panicky and had to leave the warm-up area: although the danger did not actually affect her – or indeed Billy and Jenny – it triggered a state of fear and tension in Karen which then spoilt her concentration in the test. Learning from this, she made sure she prepared many more possible scenarios before her next competition!

We can think of branch points as a way of efficient route-planning. Just as it is possible to take a train from Brighton to Bath via London or via Salisbury – or via Haywards Heath and Reading – so there are many ways in which we can arrive at our goal. If we have thought out the most likely alternative routes beforehand (and some of the less likely ones just in case), then we are not thrown and made helpless by the unexpected, but instead remain in a fit state to take charge: a state of competence.

Planning can usefully involve relating long-term and short-term, and chunking down larger goals into smaller contributing steps. It may involve drawing on the help of friends and experts. You might want to put your plans on paper. You might find it helpful to keep a diary.

> When we backed and schooled our young horse, Hawkeye, under our trainer Kimberley's expert guidance, she suggested that we keep a diary of everything we did with him. Since Leo and I and our daughter Charlotte were all involved in this, we each wrote up our own sessions with him, and for over a year kept a record of what we did, how he responded and what we thought about his progress. On a daily, weekly and monthly basis it allowed us to benchmark how we were all doing – very easy to forget when living in the moment. Since, sadly, he died at the young age of six, this record is now also a poignant but precious reminder of the special relationships that developed with him.

At this stage it can really help to flesh out our plans in the kind of detail that is powerful for us. By now you know which representational systems work most strongly for you, and have some idea of which sub-modalities within them are most influential (for example, colour *v* black-and-white, close-up *v* distance, moving *v* still, for visual). This means that you can begin to build representations of what you want as part of your planning to achieve it. Ride that half-pass, feel the lowering of the inside hind as it crosses under you, feel the swing of each canter stride as you match the suppleness if your horse's back with your own, thus amplifying it in a glorious calibration… Or picture the soft, swinging movement, hear the rhythm… NLP calls these dynamic representations **compelling futures**: in making use of our own self-knowledge to create just the very way of experiencing which *makes sense for us* we create a relationship between the future and the present that draws us compellingly towards it.

And as you create your compelling futures, use the best of what you know. Model your own skills and achievements, and also model the best of others. Again, use your strongest representations for this. If you have watched a rider with a wonderfully supple seat, how does it feel to be in their shoes? How would you look if your seat were like that – how would the world look from inside your own eyes if that was how you were riding? You can model a small chunk – a specific movement; or medium – a whole test; or large – a way of training, an attitude of mind; and you can make that part of your compelling future.

For some things, it may help you to construct a whole flow of experience: riding a test, for example, can be greatly helped if you mentally rehearse it in its full sequence.

Early on in my work with Karen, we tried to understand why she had problems learning tests. It turned out that she heard the words in her head (*Enter at A, working trot... etc*) just as she had repeated them to herself; but she is very visual and this didn't help her see her way to it... Also, she had to wait until she had nearly finished a movement before 'playing' the next set of instructions in her mind, but that was far too late to help her prepare in time. Learning to visualise the test as a connected whole, like the Yellow Brick Road in *The Wizard of Oz* was the way for her.

You may also need to rehearse variations in order to accommodate unexpected possibilities:

I remember one experienced professional rider telling a story against himself about the freestyle music programme he was about to perform in a Regional Final: he said wryly that he wasn't sure that this performance would be the same as the previous one, where he had won the Qualifying competition, because when he went into the arena the last time he found he had forgotten his own programme and had had to make it up. Being a professional, he had carried on, improvising to fit the remaining music, and no-one (except perhaps his horse) would have known. Now, though he still had his original version on paper, he didn't remember the accidental changes!

Doing

One of the most important things we can bear in mind here is that what happens is feedback not failure. Planning has given us guidelines for our doing, but if we follow them too slavishly we can compromise our ability to be flexible and so limit our effectiveness. One of the early discoveries of NLP was that the people who were the most effective and influential in any situation were the ones who had behavioural flexibility. In Chapter Four I described how this readiness to experiment is one of the four essentials of NLP – it is the E of the ROSE. All experiments need verifying, and assessing the effectiveness of what we do by comparing outcomes with aims is an essential step in this. If we are in an experimental frame of mind it is easier for us to take outcomes that in some way don't quite match our intent as feedback – then any mismatch can be helpful for improving our further planning and further actions.

Having

> The art in having, then, is in wanting what you get. This does not mean giving you what you originally wanted. The having that we are talking about here could be achieving one of the detailed steps along the way to accomplishing your overall outcome, or it could be achieving the overall outcome itself.
>
> LESLIE CAMERON-BANDLER, DAVID GORDON, MICHAEL LEBEAU *Know How*

If your outcomes have been well-formed, and your planning and actions appropriate, you should be well on the way to achieving your riding goals. And you will have flexible ways of dealing with the unexpected. So you will have much to be pleased with. A really important part of having is to make time to appreciate what it is that we do have. Allow yourself to relish each and every achievement before pressing on to the next goal. If you don't, you miss a great

'Having' –
Wendy on Lolly.

deal of pleasure and satisfaction, and deprive yourself and your horse of some of the very rewards that give you an incentive to continue.

> The experiences of having accomplished, learned or done to the best of your ability are all criteria which are evaluated and satisfied (or not) by you alone.
>
> LESLIE CAMERON-BANDLER, DAVID GORDON, MICHAEL LEBEAU *Know How*

It is great to have praise from outside: a good word from your trainer, high marks from a judge, driving home with another rosette in the window of your vehicle. It is also great – and entirely within your control – to 'take a moment' to appreciate that elevated medium trot across the diagonal you just did in an empty school. Let your horse appreciate it too; walk on a long rein for a moment so that the appreciation can be shared quietly between you. If you wait for your end-goal to arrive before praising yourself, you could both have a thinner time

Leo and Lolly 'taking a moment' to appreciate what they have just done.

than you need to. Appreciating the smaller achievements gives you many good feelings, and stronger reinforcement.

Striving for the best is a useful thing – but not if nothing less than the best will do. What if your horse doesn't ever progress beyond Novice? Should that be considered a failure if he remains soft, supple, attentive, a pleasure to ride? Only one horse can win the gold medal at the Olympics – and only every four years at that. But if we frame success differently, every rider and every horse can enjoy many of their own moments of having. As Charles de Kunffy says in *The Ethics and Passions of Dressage*, 'Do not seek arrival but enjoy the process of getting there.'

NLP at Work

Introduction

By now you will know your way around the core ideas and strategies of NLP, and hopefully have gained an idea of the variety of ways in which it can be used to help us as riders. Now it is time to look at how it works in the 'real world'.

Each chapter of this book begins with a quotation from Charles de Kunffy, whose writing and training have helped and inspired so many riders. NLP is a description of how people think and how their thinking translates into behaviour and communication. When we ask people who do things well exactly how they go about it (in other words, when we model them) we get guidelines and recipes which we can try out ourselves. I had read de Kunffy's books and watched him training for whole days at a time over a number of years. Then I interviewed him as part of a modelling project for my NLP Master Practitioner's course. *The Structure of Excellence* which follows is a kind of NLP portrait of him, and shows how many of the ideas explained under separate headings in this book come together naturally in the work of an outstanding rider, judge and trainer.

The case-studies that follow are of individual riders I have helped using NLP. In each case, NLP helped us to clarify the exact nature of their problems, pinpointed the changes they needed to make, and gave them some individually tailored strategies for the way forward.

Two of these case-studies are of friends, who also generously gave me their time in reading and commenting on the book as it grew. We have been able to spend time together not only in working on their problems, but also in exploring the exciting implications of bringing dressage and NLP together in a systematic way for the first time. I have certainly gained a great deal from this partnership: they reinforced my enthusiasm and stimulated my thinking. I have felt very supported: Karen's eloquence has provided me with wonderful ways of expressing points we wanted to share, and Nikki has paid me back in my own kind in the most delightful – and tough – way by using NLP to help me sort out stuck areas in my own riding.

The other two studies are of my husband, Leo, and myself. This whole project started when one of our trainers said to me that, despite having other relevant riding skills, Leo 'had no feel'. At that time I was just beginning my NLP training, and this judgement propelled me into thinking about the issue of 'feel' in horsemanship: how important it was, how it related to kinesthetic processing, and how it might be learnt or improved with the help of NLP. As the case-history shows, a major benchmark of our success in this was the same trainer's spontaneous comment that Leo's 'feel' had really improved.

I have also included a brief outline of the ways in which NLP has helped me, because I am an 'ordinary' rider too. I came to dressage late, and while I have been lucky enough to have excellent teachers and good horses I am not a professional; I don't have elastic finance or wonderful facilities. I do have commitment, and curiosity, and a willingness to work on myself in the service of my horse. And I believe that these are enough.

The Structure of Excellence:
Charles de Kunffy

To model a skill you focus on three neurological levels: what the
model does (their behaviour and physiology), how they do it (the
way they think) and why they do it (beliefs and values).
JOSEPH O'CONNOR AND IAN MCDERMOTT *Principles of NLP*

NLP arose from the study of excellent practitioners, and from attempting to describe exactly what they did internally and externally. This is modelling. I want to look in some detail at one outstanding equestrian in order to show how NLP can help us understand his skills and how they work.

Charles de Kunffy is an international dressage judge and trainer. His books on classical riding are well-known for their practical yet philosophical approach. He believes that, since we require the horse to carry us on his back, the weakest part of his anatomy, we owe it to him to help him develop his muscles and way of going so that he can work easily and with least damage.

For this reason, de Kunffy's work is important for everyone who loves and enjoys riding horses. A fit, well-balanced, well-schooled horse is a joy to ride out hacking, not just in competition. He is also safer, since his attentiveness and responsiveness to his rider's aids means that he will act quickly when the rider asks in an emergency (for example, in traffic). If we think of the aims and the methods of 'dressage' as belonging largely or only to one specific discipline, we miss much of what it has to offer to every horse and every rider. De Kunffy's wisdom as a writer and trainer, and the detailed NLP of how he does what he does, give us invaluable access to processes we can further develop in ourselves.

Charles de Kunffy is unique – and he is also a great exemplar of what works. In a sense he offers us both a model of excellence and an example of how one

Charles de Kunffy.

unique person goes about things. Thus it is fitting to look at him in some detail, to draw out his very personal NLP.

I have been fortunate enough to watch him on many occasions, training a range of horses at different stages of development, from newly backed young-sters through to Grand Prix. The account which follows is based both on first-hand observation and on personal interview.

A very useful concept in NLP is that of **states**. As I explained earlier in the book, a 'state' involves attitudes or beliefs as well as experience. It may be triggered intentionally, or by something occurring externally and 'accidentally'. For example, when we are pupils in any context we are likely to get into states similar to those we experienced when we were pupils in school, with similar enabling or disabling consequences. So we might feel inferior, hesitant, curious, eager, vulnerable to criticism. Or we might be observant, attentive, enjoy being shown what to do and eager to practise it.

When De Kunffy teaches, his state involves stillness and intentness, both of which are visible externally. Also, internally, there is a deliberate putting aside of self-concern in order to concentrate on his pupil. He may, for example, be tired or hungry, but so far as he is concerned the pupil at the end of a long day's teaching deserves just as much attention as the first pupil of the day.

When I asked him about this, he quoted an army saying which means that in such circumstances one should '*shut up and serve*'. Applying this maxim, he watches and listens carefully, paying attention to the horse and rider rather than to his own sensations or needs. His behaviour is guided here by his beliefs.

How does de Kunffy go about observing his pupil so accurately? When I asked him, he replied: '*I ride with them – even when I judge*'. In everyday conversation, we would think of this as a metaphor – something about feeling for the rider, perhaps. In terms of what actually happens inside his head, however, the words he uses do accurately represent what he does: he feels the experience kinesthetically, as if he were doing it. Because he 'rides with' the riders in his mind, he is able to draw on his own stored body-experience, as well as his theoretical understanding, to enrich the information and suggestions he gives them. He knows from the inside what they need to be feeling and doing because he knows what that is like.

As he told me about this, he was struck by another thought: '*When I rode, I saw myself in my mind*' (visual, dissociated processing). So he has different internal patternings for different purposes: one for teaching, one for monitoring himself.

When he reminds himself to 'shut up and serve', however, he is probably hearing the saying inside his head as part of his own internal dialogue.

It is important here to remember, although de Kunffy is outstanding, we all have the inherent ability to do the things he does. We can all remember how something feels physically, we can all make pictures in our heads, we can all hear internal sound, at least to some extent. People tend to favour one or more of these systems, and if you have been saying as you read this 'I can't/don't do that' it is probably because you tend not to use that particular system as much as the others, not because you lack the correct 'wiring' inside your head. An everyday example may help to illustrate this point. Has anyone ever told you that you walk, or talk, like one of your parents? Yes, you do carry half their genes, but the resemblance is more the result of your unconscious observing and copying of them during your childhood. Your basic physical equipment has developed in a similar way through years of experience of watching and listening, and because of their importance to you as you grew up.

Life teaches us to model unconsciously, but we can also learn to model consciously. If we observe the trainer or rider we admire intently, and ask ourselves the 'how' questions, we can help our bodies learn to put themselves into states and positions which we would like to learn from others. And because 'the hip bone is connected to the thigh bone', changes that we make in one part of the system will inevitably connect with and affect others.

This is one reason why metaphors help us. If we are told to imagine our spine as a spring, our knowledge of springs will unconsciously affect what our mind tells our body to do. The words 'think' or 'imagine' are cues to make use of our own favoured representational system. Both might signal an internal picture, or equally an internal kinesthetic experience. Either can be effectively replayed back into changes in physiology.

Good teachers like de Kunffy make use of this knowledge (which may be instinctive in good communicators) by covering all the options. While observing him I have jotted down phrases which show how he reaches all riders, whatever sensory system(s) they favour. Some comments in fact relate to more than one system:

'Your hands so close together they should be on the same steak-plate…'
'He should hang down beneath your hands.'
'I always have a visual feel that…'
'That melancholy stride I want.'

Some are primarily visual:
'When you come to review this work…'
'This is a nice composition.'

Some are kinesthetic:
'Feel what his back is telling you…'
'Sit on the coiled springs of the horse.'
'…a sitting trot…climbing uphill…'
'There should be a no-contact feel…'
'Empty your hand…'
'…massaging the horse outwards…'

And some auditory:
'The outside rein should speak forward and down.'
'The next statement you make is with both hands forward.'
'By sitting on him I can get some answers from the horse.'

These examples show how de Kunffy makes full use of the representational systems. Talking with him made it clear to me that his internal experience is similarly rich. He uses his own kinesthetic experience as he teaches and judges, and he also has a complex internal way of visualising. At the beginning of each half-hour lesson he watches the horse and rider working for only a few minutes before identifying what the lesson needs to address. I asked him what was going on in his mind.

He told me that he begins by '*Remembering the ideal, how the great things look*'. Then he asks himself '*What's missing; what's the key?*', looking for what he called a '*statement of cause*'. He described this as '*insight*', again a visual indicator. In looking for what is missing, he is literally comparing two images in his mind – an ideal and, against it, the actual movements he is watching. He described this as being like '*cellophane overlays*'. This is contrastive analysis in action. However, the process is more complex still: he sees further overlays which represent how this horse and rider need to be working in three months time (when he will see them again) and how he would like them to be at the end of the current lesson. So he has four related images to work with.

If this sounds complex, it is; but the astonishing thing is that we can all do equally rapid and complex things in our own heads. Like most people, de Kunffy had not analysed how he did what he did before I asked him. In fact, most people think that what they do is what everyone does! We use the word 'thinking' as if it had one meaning, while in fact it varies tremendously from person to person. Each of us thinks uniquely. The building blocks of thought may be the same, but the combinations are literally infinite. As you read this you may be thinking 'Oh, that's what I do, too', or realising how you do it differently. My trainer Debby, when she read this section, realised that she compares different kinesthetic 'feels' when she rides or teaches. As she rides a schooling session, she works the horse from the initial (actual) feeling he gives her towards the feeling she knows she wants to get. We could also do the same contrastive work with auditory information to improve rhythm.

The need for some improvements can be traced and dealt with primarily at a physical level. But what about physical behaviours that originate from a feeling, or a past experience, or a belief? The Logical Levels model offers us a way of identifying the origins of problems and ways of enhancing good performance.

In watching de Kunffy teach, and in reading his books, one can clearly appreciate his skill on each of the logical levels. *Training Strategies for Dressage Riders* perhaps best illustrates how his ability to use the training **environment** (both the school and the exercises within it) can work towards the goal of greater health and happiness in the horse through his increased athleticism and comfort. In all his work, addressing the specifics of **behaviour** then becomes another means towards the same end. De Kunffy's fundamental **belief** is that we owe all horses good training, and good experiences in their training, in exchange for imposing ourselves upon them. For this reason, it is also his **belief**, and an underlying assumption of this book, that classical training should be seen as the basis of all horsemanship, not as relating simply to the sport of dressage. Therefore, training should seek to improve the **capability** of both horse and rider to be most comfortably and elegantly and effectively themselves. This, in turn, respects their individual **identity**, while recognising that it goes beyond both behaviour and capability.

All good teaching rests on a highly developed ability to observe (**sensory acuity**), and de Kunffy's skill and speed in identifying and helping the rider to adjust small details of their own and their horse's behaviour is outstanding. We do all notice tiny details. In everyday life most of us easily recognise if someone we know is off-colour, depressed, anxious, cheerful, etc. – in that one word rapidly and confidently summarising a host of fine details of expression, posture, muscle tone, skin colour, and so on. We can often do the same with our horses or domestic pets. This attentive watching and attention to any changes – the NLP skills of **calibration**, **contrastive analysis** and finding the difference that makes a difference – are the means by which de Kunffy, like all outstanding trainers, can help riders make effective changes so accurately and rapidly.

I have shown how, by using metaphoric language covering the major representational systems, de Kunffy ensures that he 'reaches' all kinds of riders, even if he isn't aware of their preferred system(s). He quite literally 'talks their language'. If we are involved in teaching others, this is a skill we, too, can deliberately cultivate. Teaching a group, we can make sure we cover all the options. Teaching individuals, we have more time to pay attention to (focus on, tune in to, get a feel for) the particular person we are working with, so that we can refine our communication more closely to them.

Connecting with others, whether human or equine, depends on our ability to imagine how the world is from where they stand. This means, in other words, being willing to imagine what it is like to be the person, or horse, we are interacting with, and how our actions will seem to them. **Taking second position** in this way is one of de Kunffy's strengths as a trainer: he imagines what his effect is on the rider, and how changes in the rider will then be experienced by the horse. He is second-positioning both of them.

Empathy is one major means of building **rapport**. And rapport is one of the key features in good communication. How does de Kunffy establish rapport with his students?

- Essentially, he joins them wherever their starting point is. To begin with, he watches for a few minutes without comment. Obviously, they know that he will not leave them how he found them at the beginning of the lesson; but his silent attentiveness conveys a message of acceptance and respect. As he says,

'*Always you go through the rider*', but the message he gives through the rider to the horse is also one of acceptance.

- He makes a clear distinction between accepting the whole and criticising the part (in this case, identifying what needs improvement). Where he can see that the horse's mistake might have been caused by a misunderstanding, or by the rider's insufficiently clear aiding, he will describe it as '*an honest mistake*'.

- In saying what the rider needs to aim for, he may add '*This is not something you expect today*'. This implies a chunking down of a long-term goal into shorter-term tasks.

- He offers frequent praise: '*Do it one more time so I see it from the front…looks good*'; he may use it to soften criticism: '*Now he marches nicely and doesn't show any restlessness*'; he will also encourage the rider to give non-verbal praise to the horse by encouraging a few moments on a loose rein as a reward for concentrated work, or by stopping work on a particular exercise as soon as it has been performed satisfactorily once.

- He treats the rider as a partner, making the assumption that they have noticed the same things as he has: '*You feel the irregularity*'; '*I know you sense what I sense, but somehow the back is not participating in the canter*'; '*Don't give up, we just started!*'

In both his teaching and his written work de Kunffy stresses the importance of rapport between horse and rider. I have mentioned how he often uses the metaphors of speech – the rein '*speaking forward and down*' for example. In his book *The Ethics and Passions of Dressage*, he also shows what kind of relationship between horse and rider he values and is aiming for:

> …submission is born of trust and verified by harmony.

> The aids, the 'language of riding', can be patiently taught to a horse only by repeatedly explaining the correct responses we expect. Any understanding of communications should be rewarded to reinforce the delivery of correct responses…

> When we can induce a dance between horse and rider, we cease to command him from the outside.

> The instant willingness of the horse to respond to the imperceptible suggestions of a sophisticated rider is the very by-product of years of harmonious familiarity and the resultant attitude of joy to please.

All riding has to have a goal, because the rider has to direct the horse – even on the most mundane hack. Dressage, which aims to develop the horse's athleticism, has a complex set of interrelated goals with varying time-frames. NLP uses the word '**outcome**', rather than 'goal' because it presupposes that achievement comes out of actions taken. This is true even when the 'actions' are in the mind part of the body-mind (as, for example, in the difference I made to my feelings about cantering). A trainer like de Kunffy has to have clear outcomes for each horse-rider pair, for each session. As I have shown, one way he arrives at this is through his complex visual overlay strategy, which in turn rests upon his knowledge of correct movement and ways of developing the horse as an athlete.

Outcomes express the relationship between our wish or intent and the actions we take towards that end. And all good outcomes meet certain criteria, as I explained earlier. Good trainers like de Kunffy know what is possible at each stage of a horse's training, and also relate the individual horse-rider pair to that overall ideal. He will often explain how a particular action relates to a desired outcome.

- Working once with a horse who would not stand still in the halt but kept tossing his head, he asked the rider to repeat the halt, aiming to release the rein as a reward for stillness before, rather than after, the horse had a chance to jerk the rein again: '*I want to out-think him and release him before his first toss, because this is his anxiety syndrome*'.

- Sometimes he will comment on an outcome after it has actually been achieved, so that it becomes a reason to praise: '*He is now beginning to oil his hocks, to lubricate them*'.

- In talking with me, he described how he was always looking for '*What is possible – for example, the horse moving more freely in front – for what can be done towards that end, for what's possible in a curriculum.*'

De Kunffy constantly demonstrates sensory acuity as he pinpoints small but significant details in the horse and rider. Watching and doing are at the heart of his outstanding skill as a trainer.

The final element of the ROSE is a readiness to **experiment**. The founders of NLP recognised that, in any situation, the person with the greatest flexibility in their behaviour was most likely to influence the outcome. Behavioural flexibility involves translation – from one thought into another, one action into another, from one phraseology to another, from one strategy to another. A verbal example of this is the way de Kunffy uses many different metaphors. In doing this he ensures 'best fit' with each rider; and because many of his metaphors are unusual they also gain and retain the rider's attention. For example, a canter departure should be 'like striking a match'; a good half-pass at canter is 'like slicing a tomato'; a horse who is not 'through the back' is 'like a front horse and a back horse'. Any metaphor is an example of flexibility in the speaker's thinking, which gets the listener thinking too. In asking ourselves how a half-pass is like slicing a tomato we consider redness, roundness and seededness before fixing on the crispness of definition involved in slicing something which feels and sounds both soft and firm. Equally, the idea of slicing helps us to the notion that each stride in a good half-pass moves sideways like a slice. There is something here for everyone, whether auditory, visual or kinesthetic – and all this in milliseconds! Oddly enough, the ways in which the half-pass is not tomato-like actually help us engage with the metaphor: we have to work for it, and feel the achievement of meaning when we 'get' it.

The use of schooling movements and patterns in training is another example of behavioural flexibility in action. *Training Strategies for Dressage Riders* exemplifies a deep understanding of how patterns of movement, direction and gait within the defining space of the school can put the horse in a position in which it is natural and inevitable that he develops the correct musculature and balance. De Kunffy told me that he often changes his plan for a lesson as it goes along, as he becomes aware of changes in the relationship between ideal, desirable and possible. In a similar way, it can really help us as riders to develop a range of alternative options when we become stuck or fail to get the responses we want.

A favourite saying in NLP is that 'there is no failure, only feedback'. In changing the way we look at ' failure', we are **reframing**. When de Kunffy talks of 'an honest mistake' the apparent contradiction makes us shift the interpretation from one of blaming the horse to one of wondering how he thought that was what we wanted – a shift which has very different results in terms of what we think and do next. Similarly, when a horse is idling along, de Kunffy will often suggest the rider taps the horse with the whip as a 'wake-up call' – adding 'Go on, you know he loves it'. How could a horse 'love' a tap with the whip? This shifts the rider into wondering what messages other than punishment the action might give the horse.

I said at the beginning of this book that I believe riders want to do the best they can. Often, however, it is difficult to know where to begin. Seeking help from a trainer is one way of doing this – but then the trainer has to ask the same question. What is the starting point? With long experience as a rider and teacher, de Kunffy knows how to find the right place for intervention. For example, he may trace a problem in the horse's engagement or roundness back to the rider's

A tap with the whip – 'you know he loves it.' Vals can produce a better walk than this: the expression in his eye, to my mind, acknowledges the message, although the tap has not impaired his calmness.

leg aid; this in turn may lead him to examine the position of the leg, perhaps identifying a lack of effectiveness in the leg as originating in the ankle, since it is 'the flexibility in the ankle [that] makes you a rider that can speak to the horse'. He is asking, and answering, the characteristic NLP question **How…?**

Attention to detail allows rider and trainer to build up a better whole. Every schooling session, in de Kunffy's view, either takes the horse forward or takes him backward: no experience is neutral. I have drawn on our conversations in exploring new ways of looking at those common problems of disobedience, anticipation, evasion and anxiety in Chapter Five. De Kunffy's approach is that of the scientific investigator: he wants to know how and why the horse does what he does, rather than making judgements about 'right' and 'wrong'. Judgement on its own stops us: enquiry takes us forward.

I began this section with a quote which directs us to the What, the How and the Why. When we use NLP to help us understand how an outstanding person in any field does what they do, we begin to uncover the nuts and bolts behind what looks effortless. We find ways to learn how the person we admire does what they do, so that we can begin to do it too. This is learning of a very special kind. We do not have to feel inadequate watching a great rider and trainer: we may be awed but we are not made helpless. In fact, the opposite applies. The more information we can gather (from observation, from asking questions, from making connections), the more tools we get for working on our own. And this is true whether we are modelling people who are outstanding practitioners in many aspects of equestrianism or those who, like ourselves, are more 'ordinary' riders, good at doing just some things well.

This means that, with the help of NLP, we can actually become more skilled, or understanding, or effective versions of ourselves. Knowing the internal and external structuring of how our models do what they do well, gives us a way to go beyond imitation to a learning which becomes authentically our own, because it is in our heads, our bones, and our muscles.

Case-studies

Working with Leo

This was where it all began: a five-month project in which I began to explore how one aspect of NLP could make a difference to riding. That was some time ago; but I have left the account much as it was when I submitted it as part of my Master Practitioner Project.

Until we were given our first horse, Tristan, Leo had never ridden. He was then fifty-two. He had been a middle-distance and cross-country runner, and was fit, exercising regularly at the gym and once again running regularly. He said to himself then: '*If I am going to keep a horse I will learn to ride it*', and over time became very proficient, with a naturally good balance and a bold approach, free from the fearfulness which hampered me. Having learnt correctly from the beginning, his position and style were well-formed, and he consciously modelled himself on the upright, forward-looking stance of Arthur Kottas, the Chief Rider of the Spanish Riding School, whom he had seen riding on video, in photographs and in person. At the time I began my NLP training Leo had been riding for over seven years: we had been involved in backing and schooling a young horse, Hawkeye, as well as in riding Tristan and our other schoolmaster, Lolly. After Hawkeye's untimely death we acquired Vals, who had been backed but not schooled.

One autumn day Leo was having a lesson on Lolly, and I was watching beside our trainer, who commented that Leo's riding *lacked feel*. I felt angry and protective – but also challenged, since I was about to begin my NLP training, already knew something about representational systems and thought that NLP might be used to help Leo. It seemed to me that no one actually 'lacks feel', since we all exist kinesthetically; but I could certainly accept that someone might not be particularly cued into their kinesthetic experience.

Leo as a beginner, riding Tristan. Despite his inexperience, Leo is creating a confidence in Tristan through his correct, open body posture.

BELOW *Leo modelling Kottas, when he first began to ride.*

Our work together concentrated on helping Leo to become more aware of specific details of his kinesthetic experience while he was actually riding, whereas work with the other case-study riders was directed more towards their internal processing and how this could be used to address difficulties and make improvements.

Leo agreed to work with me on some exercises designed to help him access kinesthetic information in order to achieve particular riding tasks. We came up with a list of things he wanted to be able to do and where it seemed that greater kinesthetic awareness would help.

'Leo's riding lacked feel.' Leo with Lolly.

Leo with Lolly. Leo is overaiding with his upper body and trying too hard to organise Lolly with his hands. Lolly is overbending sideways in the neck, since the draw-reins prevent him from hollowing and coming off the bit.

- Learning to recognise which hind leg was lifting.

- Developing a habit of dropping his centre of gravity to hip level in order to secure and deepen his seat.

- Distinguishing without looking which foreleg was the leading leg at canter.

- Distinguishing without looking which diagonal he was rising to at trot.

- Learning to feel whether the horse was straight or crooked.

- Feeling without looking whether the horse was on the bit.

- Feeling if the horse was working with impulsion.

- Feeling the degree of engagement of the inside hind in lateral work.

- Assessing impulsion, rhythm and angle in shoulder-in.

- Monitoring his own shoulder positioning.

This was an ambitious list, but certainly increased kinesthetic awareness would help in every item!

Leo 'monitoring his own shoulder position'. Alignment with the horse is improving, though the left shoulder is a little dropped.

During the next month I worked on foot with Leo while he was riding, asking him to pay attention to what sensations he was experiencing and where:

- When a named hind leg was lifting under him.

- When the neck muscles were more or less relaxed.

- When he himself was bent with the horse or against the horse's movement.

- When he was still in his upper body or over-aiding.

- When he was upright or tilting to one side.

We did lots of contrastive analysis, so as to establish the key differences, and I got him to say out loud what he noticed. For example, if a rider can distinguish which hind leg is lifting, they can then use that information to:

- establish which diagonal to trot on;

- time unilateral leg aids effectively to encourage purposefulness and lengthening of stride in the walk;

- pick the most effective moment to give a specific canter aid.

Leo found he could identify the lifting leg more easily by noticing how it swung the horse's ribcage against his leg rather than by the feel of it raising his own pelvis. This may be because, like many male riders, he is not particularly supple laterally in his lumbar back. The important thing was to find a way that worked for him.

During the first month of our work together he made progress on this checklist. We noticed that he was searching more automatically for the relevant kinesthetic information, and towards the end of the second month he was commenting on kinesthetic issues as part of our informal 'debriefing' conversations on the way home from riding. What had begun in some areas as being an issue of unconscious incompetence was now something he regularly noticed without my prompting – he had become consciously competent. I noted down one example late in the second month:

> He found that when he stretched his outside leg down and back the inside knee seemed to come up. His observation about the knee was entirely his own – he did not know how he had become aware of that at that particular time – which seems to indicate that his ability to self-monitor is improving as hoped and planned.

This observation allowed us to discuss the problem of sliding to the outside, and the need to put more weight into the inside stirrup; but the fact that he had become aware himself of what was happening, rather than having it pointed out by someone else, meant that he could 'own' the corrections and make them first deliberately and then increasingly automatically.

In order to discover if this kind of work would really make an observable difference, we did not tell our teacher about it, and worked on it only when we were alone at the yard. So it was particularly confirming when, very soon after this, she said at the end of a lesson how impressed she was at Leo's 'feel'.

Learning goes on and builds on itself: in the third month since our project began Leo was recognising that, when he felt that Lolly's trot was rather bouncy, onlookers tended to tell him that Lolly was working with good impulsion. This reframed what he was feeling as 'good' rather than 'bad'; and gave him a way to tell when he was getting the kind of work he needed.

Another observation Leo made at about the same time was that he sometimes got distracted from what he was doing by having to pay attention to what our trainer was saying. The problem was not what she was saying, but rather – as we began to realise in the light of NLP – that it meant he had to pay attention to auditory information at the same time as trying to be attentive to kinesthetic. I realised that this may be a problem for many riders: since riding demands our fullest attention on an ongoing basis, the very training comments which are intended to help us may actually be giving us 'interference on audio'! This is

Leo and Lolly 'working with good impulsion'.

clearly difficult to avoid, though it suggests that riders can be helped more if they are given a quiet interval between comments in which to cue into their kinesthetic experience again and, in addition, times to practise alone what they have learnt when being taught.

Leo had learnt in a short time to improve his kinesthetic awareness. Nonetheless, it remained a less-favoured internal system for him, and it was not part of our initial project to do dismounted work to increase internal representational system flexibility. In more recent discussions, we have established that he runs internal dialogue quite significantly when he is riding: he describes to himself in a personal running commentary what he needs to be doing: '*Prepare for the turn, align the shoulders, half-halt on the outside rein*' and so on. He is also strongly visual and associated. Knowing this now, we can probably be even more effective if we add an internal 'voice-over' to help shape the work he wants to achieve. However, since riding does involve kinesthetic skill, if he wishes to develop as a rider he needs to continue to refine his kinesthetic awareness 'out there' even while largely processing it internally.

A more recent, softer version of the Kottas posture (see lower photo p.208), showing what Charles de Kunffy calls 'a well draped leg'. Despite looking too far across the circle, Leo is riding effectively and with feel, as Lolly's activity and attentive ears both demonstrate.

Leo's posture is very correct, yet his body and hands are soft, allowing Lolly to remain relatively 'uphill', even though he is on the third beat of the canter.

Working with Nikki

Nikki and I have known each other for a number of years. She is a qualified BHS Assistant Instructor, who first came to have lessons at our yard with her Thoroughbred, Fred. I remember our trainer saying then how much potential they both had, and how little confidence. Nikki had a full-time job in Human Relations and did little riding instruction, despite being qualified. After a while, Fred came to live at the yard, and later Nikki bought a young Trakehner colt, Merlin, to bring on for dressage. Sadly, Fred had incurable foot problems and had to be put down. Nikki then had a loan horse, Hooch, and later one whom she bought, Henry. Both horses were talented, but neither turned out to be an ideal match for her. Meanwhile Merlin proved strong and wilful as a stallion, had a major infection after he was gelded, and took a while to show his real talent and a more settled disposition. Nikki had a difficult time with all this, and her self-confidence took some further knocks.

Nikki was interested in what I was learning from NLP and how I was applying it to my riding, particularly since she was getting consistent messages from her trainers and from the rest of us at the yard that she was actually a good and often very effective rider with plenty of talent, and a really excellent teacher whenever she helped one or other of us with a difficulty we were having. So there was a big discrepancy between how we thought of her and how she felt about herself. She had a lifelong pattern of not putting herself forward, but her real problems of confidence went back to the time when she was doing her BHS training at a very prestigious yard, where the instructor often told her she was a 'no hoper' and would fail – mostly in front of her fellow-students. These humiliating experiences had really undermined her opinion of herself, and tended to replay in undermining internal dialogue, particularly whenever she hit a problem or put herself in a stressful situation such as a competition.

When I started to plan this book, we agreed that it would be great for us both to work together with NLP to improve her confidence, and we arranged regular dismounted sessions to tackle specific problems she and her horses were having in communicating, as well as looking at her own feelings and beliefs. We also helped each other informally at the yard, and more recently Nikki has given me some lessons, often drawing upon NLP concepts and skills.

Nikki had two central difficulties. The first was that she set herself extremely high goals, but when she failed to meet them in any way she was very critical of herself and stopped trying. The pattern actually repeated the same processes that had begun under her unsympathetic trainer, though by now Nikki had internalised his critical voice and was replaying it to herself. Internal dialogue is very

Undermined by humiliating experiences, Nikki and Fred are both 'rushing onto the forehand'. Nikki's elbows are out and Fred is hollowing and resisting the contact with an open mouth.

influential for her – and that turned out to be a key element in turning things around!

Using an NLP approach, we could see that Nikki's desired outcomes were not really well-formed, because to be outstanding as a dressage rider is not actually within anyone's realistic control. We can certainly work towards becoming as good as we can be – but that is already a very different formulation. How we benchmark our goals is also a key issue: how will we know when we have achieved them? One conversation we had showed how Nikki was effectively self-limiting over this: talking about Hooch's habit of spinning around for home when he was out hacking, she said '*If I don't conquer this I'll never ride out – and if I can't hack out why bother with horses?*'

By stacking what achieving, or not achieving, her goals meant in this way, she was building herself into a loop where one specific 'failure' could have led her to give up altogether. In fact, this problem of spinning around was one of the reasons why Nikki eventually decided Hooch was not for her – but if we had not been working on these issues she might well have decided that she was the problem, rather than him.

When she later discovered that Henry also had confidence problems, which made him afraid of being ridden in company, she was able to make the decision to sell him much more quickly and with less agonising. She had a clearer sense of the outcomes she wanted for her riding: to be able to compete, to hack out and to have fun with her horses, and she was clear that it was Henry's own difficulties, not hers, that ruled out their being able to achieve these aims together.

Nikki set herself a very high standard in her riding, and when the results didn't come up to this standard she used to become very self critical and self-blaming. If she was trying a half-pass, for example, and some aspect of it didn't work well, she would avoid doing it again. This, in turn, would affect her confidence. We explored this loop, and she was able to break out of it by setting more realistic initial goals, by reframing what happened (even if it was not quite what she wanted) as feedback and then using the feedback to guide either a reformulation of the goal or another attempt at it. As she said, the NLP presupposition *no failure, only feedback* became one she heard internally when she was riding. She was also able to use it to help her pupils when she began teaching more regularly. Using this enabling NLP presupposition, and hearing it in her internal dialogue, very effectively countered some of her old teacher's comments, which had also been processed and replayed auditorily.

The second pattern that caused Nikki problems was her habit of visualising 'ahead of herself': as she rode down the long side, for example, she could be seeing herself making a well-balanced, well-bent turn at the far end – so much so that, when she got there, she hadn't prepared and the corner in reality was neither! She said she did this in other areas of her life: in going out for a social engagement, for example, she was often so busy preparing in her head that she didn't actually allow enough time and was late.

In discussing this, we realised that this visual skill was very useful – in the right place. Visualising ahead helped her with goal-setting, but she also needed to be able to switch between imagining ahead and actually being in the experience where she was, which for her was largely kinesthetic. She needed, in other words, to get faster at changing from one representational system to another. Then she could establish a dialogue between them, using her 'here and now' kinesthetic awareness to refine and update her goal, and her visualising ahead to guide her experience here in the present. As things began to change, she said, 'I now have an ability to step outside myself [K] and look ahead again [V]'. As she became aware of the possibility of switching, and switching faster, she no longer felt trapped in either a trance-like viewing of the future which effectively disabled the present, or in aimlessly experiencing the present without relating it to a goal. She was developing a very flexible ability to change from one representational system to another, and to change back and forth between associated and dissociated viewpoints. Many other riders, I believe, would find similar switching very valuable.

Nikki was also anxious about competing, though she wanted very much to do it. Being very determined, she had made herself compete even though Fred could be quite naughty in the arena. She dreaded tests, and her husband said that he dreaded them too, because she became so withdrawn and 'inward' beforehand. During our conversations, many of which involved us in taking second position to try to understand the horse's perspective, she became convinced that, in competition, Fred's security and confidence would have been adversely affected when she lost attention. If she became absorbed in her own anxiety, she could not be there for him. His responses would then mirror her anxiety, leading to greater anxiety on her part, and a calibrated loop would result. Nikki began to remind herself (internal dialogue again) that she could do the movements at home – *therefore I **can** do this*. She became clearer about her capability in partnership with her horse, and less apprehensive about the test environment. She started to borrow our older horse, Lolly, and with Debby's encouragement went to some unaffiliated competitions, telling herself '*If I can do this on Lolly first, I'll be able to do it on other horses*.'

The effect of this was to make competition less of '*an obstacle, which gets blown up*' and more '*a process of schooling away from home*'. She was even able to say '*All I'm doing is sitting on Lolly and having a good time*'.

'We can do this.' Nickki and Lolly at Hickstead.

A number of factors helped this major transformation. Debby's support and belief that Nikki could do it, without any pressure to achieve results in the form of marks or placings; Nikki's confidence in Lolly, who in middle age is basically sensible and has done it all before, even though he can get excited and demands skill from his rider; the reframing of her goal in competing as one of *'schooling away from home'*; her newly established willingness to experiment and to use information as feedback rather than as a judgement of 'failure' or 'success'; all these worked together to make powerful changes, so that she arrived at a point where she could say *'I'm really looking forward to it'*. And of course, this Nikki was giving very different messages to her partner, so that Lolly, too, showed by his exuberance and forwardness that he was enjoying himself. Together, as a result, their performances in other competitions were good enough to qualify them for the South-East Unaffiliated Championships at Hickstead, where they produced some good work, as the photograph shows.

Nikki then bought some British Dressage tickets to compete Lolly at affiliated competitions. We all encouraged her to try him at Elementary, though she had previously only competed at Novice. Nikki was very struck by the difference which defocusing had made to Debby's posture, and began riding defocused herself. In their first affiliated Elementary test, she and Lolly achieved a mark of 58 per cent in good company, which delighted all of us (including Lolly, who loves being praised).

These changes at the levels of identity, beliefs, capability and behaviour generalised and helped Nikki in other areas of her life. She began to do more teaching, and decided to leave her current job and take part-time work in order to have time to develop as a trainer. She felt that in teaching she was passing on to her pupils many of the NLP skills she had learnt. She told me that she had found it very helpful to read the chapters of this book as they were written, and to have our regular discussions about riding issues and how NLP can help us tackle them. She felt this had helped to ingrain the learnings so that they were now second nature. Seeing the skills help her pupils had also been a powerful encouragement and reinforcement.

How has Nikki done all this? I have described how important internal dialogue turned out to be – and this was rather a surprise, since both of us had thought that her lead system was visual. But her learning, and the changes she made, involved complex interplay between all three major representational systems: adjusting the interplay between them helped her break out of some long-established patterns and begin to create the kind of riding experiences she wanted.

Recently, when we were discussing what Nikki felt NLP had helped her achieve, she said:

> The bits are coming together like pieces of a jigsaw. It's partly done and partly not – I can see some pieces coming into the slots but needing to be tweaked around to fit. But they're all there. A year ago I'd have said I couldn't see the whole jigsaw: it was like the picture on the lid of the box had been lost. Now all the edges are in place. I've seen the picture. What's it of? I honestly don't know. I could say it's a picture of a Grand Prix horse coming down the centre line, but I don't think it's true. It doesn't have to be clear. It doesn't worry me. There are lots of colours, and it's very calm. Maybe it's just waiting for me to put my authority and stamp on it.

The day before this discussion, she had enjoyed a brilliant ride on our horse Vals: alone together in the school, their rapport had been of high quality, their attentiveness to each other unbroken. This reminded us of the difference between a radio signal which is clear and 'in tune', and one which is being interrupted by interference, or blurred because it is slightly off the station: in this session Vals' and Nikki's mutual signalling had been absolutely clear, each to the other. Whatever Nikki thought of doing, her body was able to ask, and Vals was there waiting to respond. '*I just had to think of moving, and he was there*'. Shoulder-in, quarters-in, half-pass, circles and turns with lovely fluent bending, they had done them all. '*My muscles know what to do now*,' she said, 'They know what to do.' What she had learnt, as a trained teacher and committed rider, was no longer 'a rumour'.

Nikki and Merlin. 'I just had to think of moving, and he was there.'

I asked her about those long-ago sessions with her undermining trainer. *How had she experienced them? 'I can see it, hear it, feel it: all three systems. It was a bad jumping lesson. He carpeted me in front of all the others.'* Then, as she thought about it, she went on to experience a remarkable change as she used a whole range of her skills with fluency and unconscious competence to transform imprint experiences that had limited her for years.

I'm making him a figure of fun – like that rider did in your book. He's a weasely little fox. Actually I feel quite sad for him – he was quite a lonely person. There's no power there now. The picture is getting smaller – it's like a pinprick. It used to be colourful, now it's black and white. And now it's shrinking. There's no warmth or heat to it. Those experiences shrink to nothing – then there's a puff of smoke and they're gone.

A more effective posture, because Nikki is defocusing. She and Merlin are active, purposeful and in harmony with each other.

Working with Karen

This is Karen's summary of the work we did together.

To compete at a dressage competition, would conjure up the picture of a lamb being led to slaughter. My own fears and anxieties were preventing me from doing the one thing that I desperately wanted to participate in.

I had initially met Wendy in her capacity as a dressage judge (by writing for her). Following a conversation with her, regarding my problem, I was introduced to the methods of NLP as a way of helping me address my emotions.

I very soon realised, that not only did the exercises enable me to compete and enjoy the experience, but I could also adapt them to help me through everyday challenges.

Everybody has memories from the past that either consciously or subconsciously prevent them from moving forward. NLP retrieves these memories, and brings them to the forefront so that you have the opportunity to readdress them in a positive form.

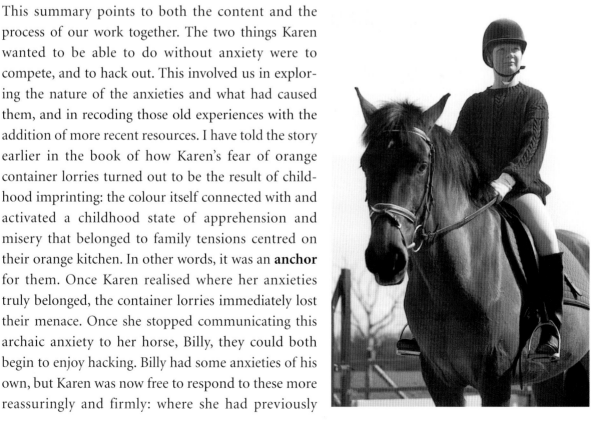

Karen and Billy.

This summary points to both the content and the process of our work together. The two things Karen wanted to be able to do without anxiety were to compete, and to hack out. This involved us in exploring the nature of the anxieties and what had caused them, and in recoding those old experiences with the addition of more recent resources. I have told the story earlier in the book of how Karen's fear of orange container lorries turned out to be the result of childhood imprinting: the colour itself connected with and activated a childhood state of apprehension and misery that belonged to family tensions centred on their orange kitchen. In other words, it was an **anchor** for them. Once Karen realised where her anxieties truly belonged, the container lorries immediately lost their menace. Once she stopped communicating this archaic anxiety to her horse, Billy, they could both begin to enjoy hacking. Billy had some anxieties of his own, but Karen was now free to respond to these more reassuringly and firmly: where she had previously looked for a convenient gateway whenever a large vehicle approached (and had on one occasion found Billy spinning round for home and dumping her in the ditch), she was now able to convince him that there was nothing to fear, and that he had better continue forwards as she asked. As a result, they have now established a regular weekend hack with a friend and her horse, which they both enjoy as a change from schooling.

As we discussed things that were happening in their schooling sessions, a number of body-work issues came up, which demonstrate how helpful NLP can be in influencing complex mind-body behaviour. The way we hold ourselves, and the way we move, also reflects how we 'feel we stand' in the world (and the everyday, often unnoticed, phrase itself tells us how we are processing this). Clear communication with our horses requires that we hold ourselves upright and that we don't look down: exploring Karen's posture also took us back to times in childhood when she had wished to be invisible, and when she had learnt to 'make herself smaller' by hunching and looking down – patterns she no longer needed in adult life. We were also able to make use of happy experiences, as in the case of the special childhood red shoes, which now help Karen's mind to keep her toes lifted.

Another body issue we worked on was that of lopsidedness. Karen became aware that she and Billy had problems on the left rein, and that her left leg was often a '*silent partner*'. As Jenny, Karen's teacher, once said to her, '*Your left leg isn't*

Lovely soft work – but a vestige of Karen's old head and shoulder posture, take her weight and Billy's forward.

talking to the horse'. Jenny has a natural ability to cue into her pupils' way of representing the world, and I am sure that matching Karen's auditory metaphor is an example.

Lopsidedness. Strangely enough, it is Karen's injured left leg which is in a deeper, more correct position while the right one is accommodating at the expense of losing depth and contact. However, she is nearly straight in her upper body, as her jacket fastening conveniently shows us, and Billy's own balance is not compromised.

We worked on Karen's asymmetry in two ways. By asking her to model how she used the two sides of her body in different areas of her life, I helped her recognise how extensive her one-sidedness was: her 'lead-leg' in walking was the right; she relied on her right hand in driving; she groomed both sides of Billy with her right hand, she carried buckets with her right hand... and so on. The practical result of this was to explore everyday, easy ways in which she could build strength (articulateness) in her left hand and leg. She bought some weights and began daily exercises, and she made conscious efforts to use her arms and legs equally whenever it was possible.

But where had the special problems with the left leg come from? When we first met, Karen had told me about a bad fall she had when jumping quite a small fence downhill: as a result she had broken her collar-bone and her pelvis. Asking her much later on in our work to connect with her left leg and let it tell her how it learnt to become so silent took her back to that fall. The fear and pain of the accident, occurring so unexpectedly as a result of a relatively small jump, had been powerfully encoded, so that even after the injuries had healed, her left side had tried to protect itself by opting out as much as possible. Thereafter, Karen sat more heavily on her right seatbone, while her left leg, hip and shoulder were less mobile, less powerful and only capable of little movements.

I asked Karen to go back in her mind to just before the accident, and to warn her body of what was coming: to tell it that it was going to be injured *but that it would make a complete recovery, as a result of which the injured side would not in future need special protection. Once recovered, it would be able to behave normally, and build its strength and skill again.* I suggested that, as this strengthening might take time, she should ask her body to tell her at any time if she was asking it to do more than it could yet manage. NLP calls this an **ecology check**: when making any change it's important to build in this kind of safety precaution to ensure that the desired change in one area doesn't produce problems in others.

As she reran the accident, watching it dissociated but with this additional knowledge, Karen felt the familiar ache in her left leg go away. The leg felt '*more relaxed, freer, without tension*'. She said it was as if the leg – once so silent – was saying '*I was hurt. Now I'm mended. Now I know you understand I'll be as mobile as I can, and let you know if I'm overdoing it*'. Karen often runs internal dialogue, so adding a reassuring internal commentary to the accident came naturally and felt right to her.

In doing this work it was important for us to respect the fact that for some years Karen's left side had been less active, and that it would take time to build strength again. Neither of us could know how long this would take, or what its capacity to become truly equal would be. We needed to be realistic, and to respect the importance of self-protection – but in a way which could also be updated. Karen's practical work in re-educating herself towards greater symmetry since our work together has shown that she certainly has much greater capacity than before; and she is safe to continue to explore how much she can do, knowing that her body will tell her if she overdoes it!

Much of our ongoing work together has concerned the quality of communication between Karen and Billy. As she once said, '*A willing partner is better than a slavish partner*', and both she and Jenny have shown an outstanding ability to get inside Billy's shoes – to take second position with him in order to establish how he experiences things and, in particular, to check out how he experiences *them*. Taking second position offers us not only the opportunity of entering into the other's world: it provides us with a mirror for our own behaviour as they may be experiencing it. In riding, as I have argued throughout the book, this is invaluable. It gives us a way of assessing the relationship between our intentions and our actions: if we take the horse's behaviour as ongoing feedback, we can use it to refine what we do and to help build positive and enriching calibrated loops.

'A willing partner.'

Karen described one such loop when she was contrasting warming up for a competition before our work started with how she warms up now. She said that, in the past, she had spent so much time trying to avoid other horses in the warm-up area that not only did she not achieve the warm-up work she had planned, but she became overloaded and panicky and actually less effective in avoiding fellow-competitors! Now, the *spiral of attentiveness to each other* that she and Billy have established meant that they were focused on their work together: strangely, this focus meant that she was more able to monitor what other pairs were doing, and modify her own plans to take account of them without abandoning her planned manoeuvres as before. NLP would explain this apparently strange phenomenon by referring to some research in the nineteen-fifties which established that the brain can process on average only seven items at any one time, plus or minus two (i.e. a range between five and nine items). While Karen was busy trying to keep an eye on all the other competitors and, at the same time, to carry out her planned warm-up – while all the time feeling panicky and anxious – she was probably well into overload. Now that she and Billy have established their mutually calibrated attentiveness, some of those available mental slots are free to monitor others. She has turned her downward spiral into a positive one.

It may also be that, as she focuses internally on Billy, she defocuses her eyes – which actually increases her ability to notice movement in peripheral vision, where our eyes are most sensitive to it. So paying less focused attention to other riders, paradoxically, may actually result in greater awareness of them!

In talking together, Karen told me that when things went wrong in riding she used to feel it was her fault. Now, since our work together, she thinks of it very differently, asking herself what has got in the way of clear communication between her and Billy. She has reframed any difficulties from what we labelled a *blame-frame* to a *curiosity-frame*. And what is in the centre of the new frame is communication. She asks herself new kinds of questions:

- What has happened in our communication? (Rapport)

- What do I really want, and can I communicate it more clearly? (Outcomes)

- How did we go? What exactly happened? (Sensory Acuity)

- What else could I do? (Experimentation)

Where the blame-frame closes things down, the curiosity-frame directs us to the principles of the ROSE – and through them to a host of possible ways forward. In this frame, she now understands Billy's evasions as questions, which it is up to her, with Jenny's help, to try to answer.

From this stance, schooling has acquired a new meaning for Karen and Billy. As she said:

> Schooling should be exciting. It's not going round in circles. It's the process of communicating with your horse. It should be fun and exciting. It's talking to your horse. If you think 'here we go again…' your own body language tells your horse it's a chore. Focus on the process means every moment is interesting. Where you used to say 'I want to tell you about shoulder-in', and the horse thought 'Not the one about shoulder-in again…' Now he says 'I like the one about shoulder-in. Tell me it again.'

Recently, Karen and Billy began to enjoy having this kind of conversation during competition, and they were placed for the first time. Now Karen is looking forward to the beginning of a new competition season. But as she says, NLP has also 'spilled over' into other areas of her life.

It's like doing a recipe for the first time. As you use the recipe more and more, you don't need to measure, and you add little bits to make it more interesting. The principles of NLP are like a recipe book. But once you've got the book, the possibilities are endless. And that's what makes it special.

NLP and My Own Riding

The life of an equestrian involves one's personal inner life and values, and one's ethics and character traits.

CHARLES DE KUNFFY *The Ethics and Passions of Dressage*

This book came into being because NLP helped me so much in my own riding. The Practitioner and Master Practitioner courses I did were ones in which the learning was experiential, in the muscle: we learnt by doing. And in doing, we worked on issues, challenges and problems from our own lives. I noticed that each time we worked together in pairs or groups I wondered what my 'problem' would be; and mostly it was something from my riding life. NLP helped me, notably, with my fear of cantering and with breaking down the goals for building my working relationship with Vals into the five stages from Present State to Desired State, both of which have been described earlier in the book.

But as I reflected, during this period of intense excitement and involvement, on what I was learning and how it was affecting my life, I was struck most of all by how the principles of good communication between people could also be applied to good communication in riding; and that was where the idea of the book began: to share with other committed riders a body of concepts and skills which could be as helpful to them as they were being to me.

My learning, of course, didn't stop at the ending of the course, or the beginning of writing the book. As I have been working on it, and sharing the ideas on a regular basis with Karen, Leo, Nikki, our trainer Debby and other friends and riders, NLP has been a tool in daily use with my own riding, as with theirs. So this brief summary of how it has helped me is, like the other case-studies, a statement of 'work in progress'.

Ever since I started riding when I was ten, I have been torn between two very powerful forces: on the one hand an absolute determination to ride, to learn, to become better, and on the other a fearfulness which meant that as a teenager I could never eat on Saturdays (riding day), spent half my time in the loo and the other half almost rigid with tension. Yet I truly loved riding, loved most of the horses and ponies I rode, made myself take every opportunity for hacking, galloping and jumping and even of riding a horse known to rear.

Perhaps the first major triumph achieved with NLP was to set my well-grounded fearfulness of cantering to rest. I'm unlikely to become a bold eventer or to wish to risk my life and that of my horse again on busy roads; but I no longer feel that build-up of tension every time I go to the yard, though I do still feel the sense of achievement, even triumph, after a good ride, and I still repeat its peak moments afterwards in quite intense kinesthetic recall. And I love the feeling of cantering!

The second major result of working with NLP was more generalised: I have been a pupil all my riding life. I have always taken lessons – latterly with Kimberley and Debby, who are talented, knowledgeable and inspiring teachers. I have spent days watching Kottas and de Kunffy teaching highly proficient riders on talented horses. I have learnt from many able and outstanding judges, both formally on courses and informally through sitting in, writing and through colleaguely conversations. I have read the experts. All of this has given me a great deal – but it has also underscored a pupil state in me. In a variety of ways NLP has helped me to recognise and grow into a sense of my own expertise, both in understanding and in actual proficiency. When I access this state, I ride better, even when being taught. I have always been a 'good pupil' – and in all the other skills I have learnt there has come a time when I have moved into an ownership of my own abilities. NLP has helped me build my confidence as a rider, as an owner and as a judge. Learning from others with more knowledge, more expertise and more skill now does not now automatically anchor me – as it used to – into feeling unsure about my own abilities.

More recently, I have recognised something else about the importance of states for my riding. Having a lesson one day on Lolly, whom I ride rarely nowadays, I found us playing with what we could do together: walk to halt to rein-back to canter; simple changes; canter half-passes; finally canter to halt. All with the lightest, most attentive, joyous communication between us. (Lolly was actually so pleased with himself, and so aware that I was pleased with him, that he kept turning in to the centre of the school after he had accomplished a manoeuvre to ask Nikki for a pat – until she and I decided we didn't want this to become too much of a habit!)

Nikki commented that when I ride Vals I try too hard. As I thought about this contrast afterwards, I realised that when I ride Lolly I ride in a play-state; when I ride Vals I ride in a schooling state. A play-state, for me, means I am saying '*Let's see what we can do*', whereas a schooling state means '*Let's try to…*'. The next time I rode Vals, I made sure that I began by thinking myself into a play-state. Debby happened to be teaching someone else in the school at the same time, and commented that our work was softer, more elastic, more expressive than she had ever seen it: we were both so much more relaxed. Accessing a play-state rather than a schooling state had created a different kind of calibrated loop, where each of us reflected and amplified the softness and freedom we felt from the other.

Wendy and Vals in pupil state – correct, but stiff and joyless. My chin has reverted to its former trying-to-see-better posture, and my waist has collapsed.

Pupil state: Wendy and Vals, with trainer and audience. Still trying hard, but a little more relaxed. However, I have come behind the vertical and Vals has ceased to be 'through' in the neck.

Play state: Wendy and Lolly. The postures and the faces say it all.

Wendy and Lolly. Another study of play state.

The third major learning concerned my beliefs, and how these affected my relationship with Vals. As I have shown in more detail earlier in the book, I used to attribute my difficulties in riding him (specifically, in getting him to go forward and in establishing a harmonious relationship with him through the rein) as ones of capability: mine: not enough.

For a long while, my trainers had been telling me to send him onward more, and to ride him into a shorter frame, but this felt uncomfortably dominant: it simply 'wasn't me'. I saw it, I now realise, as an issue of identity – so no way was I going to compromise one of the things I most value about my relationships with others; my belief in accepting and encouraging them, in their style, in their way and at their pace.

I really have Nikki to thank for turning my NLP tables on me, and asking me quite bluntly what I thought Vals was making of my behaviour. She made me take second position, in just the way in which the book is asking you, its readers, to do with your horses. And only then was I able to 'get inside' how it might be to experience my 'permissive' (inconsistent) contact and my gentle (indecisive) leg-aiding. One repeating area of difficulty Vals and I have had involved our contact. In my present-state-to-desired-state exercise, I specified that the contact I desired would feel like 'holding hands'; but I couldn't find a way to help us get there. In one lesson with Nikki I was trying to make a transition from walk on a long rein to walk on a contact, and took in a half-hearted few inches, knowing that the rein would still be too long, and saying to Nikki that I felt that, because I didn't want to provoke Vals into a resisting neck and jaw, I was '*creeping up on him*'. Nikki said immediately: '*I think it's really sad to hear you saying that. What do you think that's like for him?*' And I thought: if someone is creeping up on you what does it mean? *It means that something unpleasant is going to happen.* And that was a really powerful reframe, with profound and lasting consequences.

I had thought my difficulties were ones of capability – I wasn't really a good enough rider for my talented horse. Through Nikki's inspired use of NLP, I suddenly realised that the issue was one not of capability but of belief. I have plenty of capability – but my beliefs were getting in the way of my using it. Once I had a way to imagine Vals' experience of my aiding, I knew how much clearer and more helpful he would find me if I was decisive and consistent. In fact, I had been mistaken about the kind of behaviours that would put my beliefs into practice. Believing that the rider's job is to 'cheer up' the horse and facilitate the development of his full potential, I had unwittingly imposed on my horse (who, as de Kunffy reminded me, has no goal of his own for being ridden) an agenda for self-development that is entirely inappropriate to him, however appropriate it may be to human beings. Once I saw and felt how this might be for him, I could behave very differently to express the same beliefs – and to achieve the same aims with much greater ease and harmony.

A fourth area in which NLP has helped me is in defining the goals I have in my riding. What do I want? To be able, one day, to ride all the Grand Prix movements, preferably with Vals.

Is this a well-formed outcome?

Yes, it is *stated positively*.

Do I know the *specifics* of how it will be when it is achieved?

Yes. It will feel right, and look right, and sound right. And I know enough – and will continue to learn more – about what 'right' means in this context.

Is it within my *control* to start and maintain the process?

Yes, if I am prepared to work at my part of it and to do my part under Debby's instructions to help Vals with his.

How, when and where will it happen?

It is an achievement that can happen at home, with just the two of us, or with friends watching. It isn't about competition, it's about communication, so far as I am concerned. It is what I have wanted ever since I started to learn dressage.

Does it *maintain rather than threaten anything positive* about our current behaviour?

Now it does, now that I have sorted out the belief/behaviour issue.

Are its costs *acceptable?*

Well, I'm not going to drive myself, or Vals, to achieve this. There isn't a time-limit. It doesn't have to happen all at once. Maybe we will never get to do all of it. The process of getting there is going to be fun in itself, and losing fun, losing the enjoyment of our communication, would mean that, even if we did the movements, we would not have achieved the goal. It's the harmony and clarity of the conversation needed to achieve those movements with fluency and mutual delight that I want, and that I'm working towards. I think that's a well-formed goal.

Finally, NLP has helped me realise that, though I thought my lead system was visual, in fact much of what I treasure about riding is kinesthetic. The first time

'…the harmony and clarity of the conversation…' This picture shows Wendy and Vals in such a moment of complete mutual attentiveness. Vals is producing a huge overtrack in the walk without losing balance, and the connection through the reins did indeed feel 'like holding hands'.

I tried canter to walk on Vals, I remembered watching Charles' advanced pupils, and how they had first collected the strides so the transition went *canter, canter, plop*; I replayed this in my head as I prepared, and we went *canter, canter, plop*. Any time I want to, I can enjoy in my mind Vals' trampolining, elevated, carrying trot, the power of his neck 'hugging' me around my waist as I groom him, or Lolly's lightness and mobility off the leg in lateral movements. And I can still feel Hawkeye's huge-striding walk underneath me, several years after his death. I can enjoy those moments twice: out there in the world, and afterwards whenever I want to, in here in my head. I can make even more of that, now that I know what I am doing.

Conclusion

Riding is a process that is never finished. As a conversation between two living beings, it has many variations and brings many challenges. NLP offers us invaluable, practical, user-friendly tools for understanding and working with ourselves and others, so its potential assistance to us, likewise, is never exhausted. Not least, it can help us keep forever in our own internal representations those moments when we and our equine partners really did get it all together.

Epilogue

I am not a 'horsy' person, I do not own a horse and I have only ridden but a handful of times in my life – but I have found *Schooling Problems Solved with NLP* compelling reading.

What has gripped my attention is the extraordinary way in which the NLP understanding I teach of how to work successfully with people, groups and organisations is so readily transferable to inter-species communication.

NLP seeks out models of excellence in all walks of life. Once we think we know just how they get outstanding results, the test is to be able to teach these specific techniques to others so that they, too, may excel. So often though, it is not just a matter of skills to learn but a way of thinking and a set of beliefs that inform excellent practice. In truth it is a way of being.

I was once asked in a Master Class what single piece of advice I would offer to NLP Practitioners who had taken their training, and knew how to use what they had learnt. I was slightly surprised to hear myself say: 'When you're working with people just get out of their way so that they can do what they've always been capable of anyway.'

Equestrian excellence, it seems to me, requires the rider to do precisely this. And it offers us a wonderful opportunity for understanding how to operate in the world and engage with others of our own species. For excellence presupposes an extraordinary quality of relationship between horse and rider. And that relationship is based on a high level of rapport.

Reading Wendy Jago's book it is clear that horse and rider are engaged in a collaborative endeavour in which, if they are to be truly successful, they will need to stop trying and let go so that the internal resources of each can be effortlessly brought into play. And play is what it will be, not competitive 'command and control'. As I have found in my work using NLP, achieving such a flow state takes one far beyond mechanical practice and conscious instruction.

When working with people it frequently seems to me that they need to establish a greater level of rapport with themselves if they are to make the changes which they seek: struggle on the inside prevents them from being able to achieve success on the outside.

So what is rapport? NLP defines rapport as the establishment of a mode of cooperative communication between one or more parties. This cooperation redefines our everyday understanding of leadership: it is not enough for the leader (or rider) to decide how things will be done. No, the leader (or rider) must learn to look, listen and follow the lead provided by those they would seek to influence.

Influence then requires rapport. In equestrian matters, I would suggest, the sign of a true master is that they have the skill and awareness to influence. How do they do this? They take their lead from the horse. So who's influencing whom? In truth horse and rider influence each other. It is as if they are part of a larger system which is both of them together and more than either of them separately.

Training based on such understandings – be it to achieve personal, organisational or equestrian excellence – works on the presupposition that the wisdom to excel is already within and merely needs to be engaged and unleashed. It is as if the organism has its own self-organising intelligence which we must learn to honour and follow even as we lead toward the goal we have set. And that organism may, for instance, be a child, our own unconscious, a team, or a horse.

Wendy Jago has used NLP to model Charles de Kunffy. Her excellent account certainly offers lessons on how one could ride better, but ultimately what I take away is something more. For at its best, like any art, the equestrian art touches on that most profound art – the art of living. It is a vehicle to teach us how we might live with greater ease and accomplishment in – or out of – the saddle.

IAN MCDERMOTT
Director of Training, International Teaching Seminars

Taking it Further...

For more information, coaching and training you can contact:

Wendy Jago,
11 West Hill Street,
Brighton,
East Sussex BN1 3RR

Tel. and fax: 01273 326134
e-mail: wendyandleo.jago@virgin.net

Ian McDermott,
International Teaching Seminars,
19 Widegate Street,
London E1 7HP

Tel: +44 (0)20 7247 0252
Fax: +44 (0)20 7242 0242
Internet: www.itsnlp.com

Charles de Kunffy
Internet: www.charlesdekunffy.com

Training the Teachers of Tomorrow, Trust,
Garden Cottage,
East Whipley Lane,
Shamley Green,
Surrey GU5 0TE

Tel: 01483 272445
Fax: 01483 268371
Internet: www.tttrust.freeserve.co.uk

Further Reading

Charles de Kunffy, *The Athletic Development of the Dressage Horse: Manège Patterns*, Howell Book House 1992

Charles de Kunffy, *The Ethics and Passions of Dressage*, Half Halt Press 1993

Charles de Kunffy, *Training Strategies for Dressage Riders*, Howell Book House 1994

Joseph O'Connor and Ian McDermott, *Principles of NLP*, Thorsons 1996

Index